THE LINE OF SHEM & THE SEED OF JUDAH

The women and men who carried the line until the Arrival & Coronation of Yeshua Hamashiach

Stephen Hanks

Dedicated to Laurence "Laurencio" Gregory

The Line of Shem & The Seed of Judah
Copyright 2024 by Stephen Hanks All Rights Reserved

No part of this publication may be reproduced, stored in a retrieval system or transmitted, in any form of by any means – electronic, mechanical, photocopying, recording, or otherwise – without prior written permission from the publisher, except for the inclusion of brief quotations in a review.

For more information about this title or to order other books, contact the publisher:

Stephen Hanks
Shankbibletalk@yahoo.com
Youtube.com/Portrait Pioneers of Color

ISBN: 978-1-7366786-2-6 (Paperback)

Printed in the United States of America

Cover and Interior design:
Van-garde Imagery • van-garde.com

Contents

Chapter 1	The Beginning of the Foretold Seed	1
Chapter 2	Preparing the Ark for the Seed of Judah	5
Chapter 3	The River of Eden	21
Chapter 4	Biblical & Historical References to African Jews & Israelites	27
Chapter 5	Biblical and Historical References to African & Arab Hebrews	61
Chapter 6	King Solomon's Mines	67
Chapter 7	Shem & Ham In the Land of China	79
Chapter 8	The Five Daughters of Manasseh & Sheerah of Ephraim	101
Chapter 9	The Relief of Lachish	109
Chapter 10	How the Hebrew Scrolls Foretold the Coming Mashiach	117
Chapter 11	Historical Evidentiary Support Yeshua Is Foretold Messiah	127
Chapter 12	Christendom's Conspiracy to Enslave Descendants of the Seed	131
Chapter 13	The Real Reason Columbus Took His Third Voyage	145

Chapter 14	Black Jews Brought to America During Slavery	 151
Chapter 15	The Coronation of Messiah the Seed of Judah	 173
Chapter 16	What Do We Need to Do to Be Saved?	 191
	Notes/Sources	203
	Requested Photo Credits	219

CHAPTER 1
The Beginning of the Foretold Seed

GENESIS 3:15 And I will put enmity between you and the woman and between your Seed and her Seed. He will crush you in the head, and you will strike him in the heel."

אוּה הָעְרַז וּיבֵּו הָעְרַז וּיבֵּו הָאשָּׁה וּיבֵּו הָנִיבֵּ מיִשָׂא הַבָיֵא
."בְּקֵעָבַ וֹתו עַצַפְּתָּ הָתָּאןַ דְּשָׁאר תֵא חֲמִי

This prophetic utterance in the garden of Eden, recorded in scripture many millenniums ago, has proven to be not only the most profound statement ever spoken to mankind, but continues to be relevant today at this critical hour.

Viewed as the very first divine prophecy of God that appears in the Tanakh and the Bible, this futuristic statement is referring to events being fulfilled before our very eyes right now, and will continue to unfold during each new generation that comes along, no matter how old the book you are now holding in your hands becomes, until each & every last word of the prophecy becomes completely fulfilled.

There are two primary groups of people who need to understand the decoding of this divine cryptic prediction: those who were invited from all nations to hear, and those who were originally invited from the beginning – namely, the original Twelve Tribes of Israel, including all of their lineage, many whom were not only descendants of Shem, but also of Cush and Ham, as this book will reveal.

Thus, both groups – those of every tribe and people – and those who descended from the original people – must be given an opportunity to understand this prophetic life-saving message sent from the Most High. Right now as we speak, there are a people lost, who never were told the full story. The obligation of this book is to attempt to tell that story – the full story – so that a lost people can be found. And the way they can be found is by understanding what happened many millenniums ago, which caused the Most High to utter this prophecy in the first place.

From the *Line of Shem* – to the *Seed of Judah* – there was a coming "Seed" which had to be protected at all cost, because one family line would be entrusted with producing the *Messiah, Hamashiach* – who holds the key to our understanding the final fulfillment of this cryptic prophecy, and of the world-shaking events that are soon to take place.

Additionally, there is another prophecy from the Most High which plays a major role and bearing on that first prophecy in Eden, as it involves another symbolic woman, and will be examined in Chapter 15:

> **Revelation 17:6** – "And I saw that the woman was drunk with the blood of the holy ones and with the blood of the witnesses of Yeshua."

So here is the full story – as told by historical evidence, old world maps, word language etymology, ancestral genealogy, ancient African/Arab trade routes, African/Asian archives, ancient historians, Hebrew & Greek scripture texts, archaeological findings, and recent world news developments.

Questions that will be answered:

What Biblical references show Africans as part of the 12 Tribes of Israel?

How did ancient Ethiopia hear about the covenants of the Most High?

How does the Relief of Lachish add to the evidence of Jews descended from Ham?

What was recorded about Yeshua in the official Roman archives of Pontius Pilate in the first century CE?

What was the *real reason* why Christopher Columbus took his third voyage?

What other evidence is there about the source of King Solomon's gold?

Who sanctioned the slave trade in Africa, and what shocking event does Revelation say will happen to this class very soon?

How were the Hebrew prophecies about the Messiah fulfilled in the first century CE?

How will the prophecy about the Seed be fulfilled in the last days of the world?

And many other questions that will be answered.

Let us now begin this journey, and see where the facts lead us.

CHAPTER 2

Preparing the Ark for the Seed of Judah

> "Shem, son of Noah, son of La′mech, son of Me·thu′se·lah, son of E′noch, son of Ja′red, son of Ma·ha′la·le·el, son of Ca·i′nan, son of E′nosh, son of Seth, son of Adam, son of God." (Luke 3:36-38)

Eden's fruit trees were all there for man to eat from "to satisfaction." (Genesis 2:16) But one tree, that "of the knowledge of good and bad," was placed off limits for the human pair. Eve quoted Yehovah's prohibition given to her husband as including even the 'touching' of the tree, with the penalty of death to result from disrespect for and violation of the divine law. As to what type of the tree, the scriptures do not say. But it was not the tree itself that was important. What was important was what the tree symbolized. The tree of the knowledge of good and bad symbolized the divine right of the Most High God to determine to his perfect human and angelic creatures what is "good" and what is "bad," because it is the Most High's right to set forth His standards since He was the One who created them, gave them life. As the Sovereign Ruler of the universe, Yehovah had created perfect humans and angelic creatures with the attribute of freedom of choice. So they were given the ability to decide whether to choose to obey or not obey the Most High's laws. However, if they chose not to obey, that choice would come with consequences. But again, the Creator gave all of them the freedom to decide their actions. The Most High did not create robots, which are only made to operate only according to how they are programmed. The Most High did not want blind obedience; He desired that His human and angelic creatures worship and follow Him out of love alone. So in regards to the tree, any act of disobedience in eating its fruit would constitute the original sin and result in imperfection, leading to literal death.

From the scriptures we know what transpired. One of the Most High's angelic creatures chose a path of jealousy and self-importance, and ***turned himself into a Satan, a resister against the Most High.*** That rebel tricked Eve into eating the fruit on the tree by twisting the words of the Most High's command. The rebel also in effect slandered the Most High's name. The rebel, Satan, implied that the Most High had lied to them. But actually, Satan was the one deceiving them. Eve later offered to Adam the fruit from the tree, which he ate likewise. So two perfect humans chose to disobey the Most High. Thus, imperfection and death came upon the children of Adam and Eve and all their descendants. But everything was not to be lost. The Most High uttered a prophecy about a Seed that would come.

The first child born on earth to Adam and Eve was Cain. Following the birth of Cain, Eve said: "I have produced a man with the aid of Jehovah." (Genesis 4:1) Did she have in mind that she might be the foretold woman who would produce the seed by means of which deliverance would come?

The second son of Adam and his wife Eve was Abel, the younger brother of their firstborn son, Cain. It is probable that, while yet alive, Abel had sisters; the record mentions the birth of daughters to his parents, but their names are not recorded. (Genesis 5:1-4) As a man, Abel became a herder of sheep; his brother, a farmer.

After an indefinite period of time, Abel made an offering to Yehovah God. Cain did likewise. Each brought of what he had: Abel, of the firstlings of his flocks; Cain, of his produce. They both had belief in God. They undoubtedly learned of Him from their parents and must have known why they all were outside the Garden of Eden and denied entry to it. Their offerings indicated a recognition of their alienated state and of their desire for God's favor. God expressed favor toward Abel's offering but not Cain's. Abel's offering of the firstlings of his flock met God's approval.

The manner in which the distinction between the approved and the disapproved offerings was made is not stated, but it was undoubtedly evident to both Cain and Abel. Yehovah, who reads the heart of man, knew the wrong attitude of Cain. He chose to ignore God's counsel to get the mastery over the sinful desire that 'lurked at the door,' craving to dominate him. (Genesis 4:6, 7) This disrespectful course was "the path of Cain."

In the field Cain attacked Abel, killing him, and thereby becoming the first human murderer. Cain went into banishment in "the land of Fugitiveness to the east of Eden," taking with him his wife, an anonymous daughter or granddaughter of Adam and Eve. (Genesis 4:16, 17)

Next came Seth, the third son. Eve named him Seth because, as she said, "God has appointed another seed in place of Abel, because Cain killed him." Noah descended from Seth, not from the murderous Cain.

Enoch was the son of Jared, the great-great-grandson of Seth, the seventh man in the genealogical line from Adam. As a prophet of Yehovah, he foretold God's coming with His holy myriads to execute judgment against the ungodly. (Jude 14, 15) Likely persecution was brought against him because of his prophesying. However, God did not permit the opposers to kill Enoch. Instead, Jehovah "took him," that is, cut short his life at the age of 365, an age far below that of most of his contemporaries. Enoch was "transferred so as not to see death," meaning the Most High did not allow Enoch to be killed.

Methuselah, the Son of prophet Enoch, was of the eighth human generation. (Luke 3:37, 38) He enjoyed a life span of 969 years, the longest of Bible record, and, one that has become proverbial for longevity.

Lamech was the son of Methuselah. Then came Noah (Rest; Consolation) the son of Lamech and tenth in line from Adam through Seth; born in 2970 BCE. When his father Lamech named Noah, he said: "This one will bring us comfort from our work and from the pain of our hands resulting from the ground which Jehovah has cursed" (Genesis 5:28-31). **"The Nephilim proved to be in the earth in those days**, and also after that, when the sons of the true God continued to have relations with the daughters of men and they bore sons to them, they were the mighty ones who were of old, the men of fame"(Genesis 6:1-4). The context of verse 4, conclude that **the Nephilim were not angels**, but were the hybrid offspring resulting from materialized angels having intercourse with the daughters of men. The Greek Septuagint also suggests that both the "Nephilim" and "mighty ones" are identical by using the word gi′gan·tes (giants). Yehovah determined that he was going to end his patience with men after 120 years.

The sons of God mentioned at Genesis 6:2, therefore, must have been angels, spirit "sons of God." This expression is applied to angels at Job 1:6; 38:7. This view is supported by Peter, who speaks of "the spirits in prison, who had once been disobedient when the patience of

God was waiting in Noah's days" (1 Peter 3:19, 20). Also Jude writes of "the angels that did not keep their original position but forsook their own proper dwelling place" (Jude 6). Angels had the power to materialize in human form, and some angels did so to bring messages from God. But heaven is the proper abode of spirit persons, and the angels there have positions of service under the Most High (Daniel 7:9, 10). To leave this abode to dwell on earth and to forsake their assigned service to have fleshly relations would be rebellion against the Most High's laws, and perversion.

The Bible states that the disobedient angels are now "spirits in prison," having been 'thrown into Tartarus' and "reserved with eternal bonds under dense darkness for the judgment of the great day." This seems to indicate that they are greatly restricted, unable again to materialize as they did prior to the Flood. (1 Peter 3:19; 2 Peter 2:4; Jude 6)

The Most High chose Noah and his family to build an Ark. The Ark was a rectangular chest-like vessel presumably having square corners and a flat bottom. It needed no rounded bottom or sharp bow to cut rapidly through the water; it required no steering; its only functions were to be watertight and to stay afloat. It would be stable, and would not easily capsize. In size the ark was 300 cubits long, 50 cubits wide, and 30 cubits high. Conservatively calculating the cubit as 44.5 cm (17.5 in.), the ark measured 133.5 m by 22.3 m by 13.4 m (437 ft 6 in. × 72 ft 11 in. × 43 ft 9 in.), less than half the length of the ocean liner Queen Elizabeth 2.

The Most High instructed Noah: "Make for yourself an ark from resinous wood. You will make compartments in the ark and cover it with tar inside and outside." Noah must have built the ark in a locality where there was plenty of gopher wood on hand, in order to construct the vessel according to Yehovah's directions. It also would require faith, because Noah was to build it on dry land. The scriptures do not indicate that Noah built the ark near a river.

Yehovah set a time limit for the existence of that ungodly world, saying: "My spirit shall not act toward man indefinitely in that he is also flesh. Accordingly his days shall amount to a hundred and twenty years." (Genesis 6:3) This was a divine judicial decree. About 20 years after that, Noah's first son was born (2470 BCE), and the record shows that **another son, Shem, was born two years later.** The time of Ham and Japheth's births are not stated, but these three sons were grown and married when the divine instructions were given to Noah to build the ark. It is likely that only 40 or 50 years then remained before the Deluge (Genesis 6:13-18). Noah's father Lamech died about five years before the flood. Noah's grandfather Methuselah died in 2370 BCE, the year of the flood, but not that he lost his life in the flood. The scriptures simply say that Methuselah "died."

Seven days before the floodwaters began to fall, Yehovah instructed Noah to gather the animals into the ark. Soon the rain began. **The Most High's plan and purpose was to preserve the Line of Shem for the coming Seed of Judah.** Noah and his family carried the history of creation. After about one year in the ark, Noah and his family came out onto an earth freshly washed clean. **The ark had come to rest in the mountains of the Ararat Range.** Noah later lived out the days of his life, and died about two years before the birth of Abraham. He therefore got to see Yehovah's judgment on the builders of the Tower of Babel and the scattering of those rebellious ones over the face of the earth.

It is interesting that in history, certain tribal people in several countries preserved traditional celebrations about the Flood by observing in November a **'Feast of Ancestors'** or a **'Festival of the Dead.'** Such customs reflected a memory of the destruction caused by the Deluge. The festival in Mexico was held on the 17th of November because they "had a tradition that at that time the world had been previously destroyed; and they dreaded lest a similar catastrophe would, at the end of a cycle, annihilate the human race. This festival of the dead is held on or about the very day on which, according to the scriptural account, the Deluge took place, "viz., *the seventeenth day of the second month*"

As Genesis 7:11 stated:

> "In the 600th year of Noah's life, in the second month, on the 17th day of the month, on that day all the springs of the vast watery deep burst open and the floodgates of the heavens were opened."

That Hebrew second month, "Heshvan" corresponds to the latter part of October and the first part of November on our calendar.

Such a cataclysm as the Deluge, which washed the whole world of that time out of existence, would never be forgotten by the survivors. They would talk about it to their children and their children's children. For 500 years after the Deluge, Shem lived on to relate the event to many generations. He died only ten years before the birth of Jacob. Moses preserved the true account in Genesis.

One of the first cities to be built after the Flood was Babel. Here God "confused the language of all the earth." (Genesis 11:9) Babel, or Babylon, was the beginning of the kingdom of wicked Nimrod, the "mighty hunter in opposition to Jehovah," in the land of Shinar (Sumer). **Here the tower of Babel was a religious tower, not to be dedicated to the Most High, but for the purpose of making a "celebrated name for themselves."** (Genesis 11:4)

The time of when this false religious city was built may be drawn from what the scriptures say about Peleg, who lived from 2269 to

2030 BCE. His name meant "Division," for "in his days the earth was divided", meaning the people could not communicate anymore in the Hebrew language, since Yehovah changed their language and "scattered them from there over all the surface of the earth." Noah and Shem were not involved in the building of the tower, and consequently would not have suffered the confusion of their language, but would continue to speak man's original language, which the Most High gave to the first man. A text of Sharkalisharri, king of Agade (Accad) in patriarchal times, mentions his *restoring* a temple-tower at Babylon, implying that such a structure existed prior to his reign. (See Notes)

Let us now closely examine other names in the line of Shem.

Luke 3:31-34

"David, which was the son of Jesse, which was the son of Obed, which was the son of Boaz, which was the son of Salmon, which was the son of Nahshon, Which was the son of Amminadab, which was the son of Ram, which was the son of Hezron, which was the son of Perez, which was the son *of Judah*, which was the son of Jacob, which was the son of Isaac, which was the son of Abraham."

Judah the kingdom, which came from…
Judah the tribe, which came from…
Judah, the son of Jacob.

Because Jacob favored his son Joseph, the child of Rachel, this caused in Judah and his brothers a jealous hatred of Joseph. Their hate grew even more intense when Judah and his brothers learned that Joseph had two dreams predicting he would become superior to them. Judah and his brothers plotted to kill Joseph. However, Judah convinced the others that, instead of murdering Joseph, to sell him to the Ishmaelite merchants.

Later, Jacob sent ten of his sons, including Judah, to Egypt for food. By now, Joseph was appointed by Pharaoh as Egypt's food administrator. Joseph recognized his brothers, but they did not recognize him. Joseph accused them of being spies and warned them not to return without their brother Benjamin. After returning to their father, and explaining the situation, Jacob was unwilling to send Benjamin, his lastborn, with his other sons to Egypt. Benjamin's mother Rachel had died while giving birth to him. Judah finally succeeded in getting his father's consent and promised to be surety for Benjamin.

Joseph tested his brothers by having his steward accuse them of theft, the stolen item planted in Benjamin's bag. Judah pleaded in behalf of Benjamin. Judah even requested that he be kept as a slave in Benjamin's place. When Joseph heard Judah's offer he could no longer contain his emotions, and identified himself as their lost brother Joseph. After forgiving them for having sold him into slavery, Joseph instructed his brothers to get their father Jacob and return to Egypt.

On his deathbed, Jacob uttered a prophecy concerning his son Judah:

> **"The scepter will not turn aside from Judah, neither the commander's staff from between his feet, until Shiloh comes; and to him the obedience of the peoples will belong."** (Genesis 49:10)

In pronouncing a blessing upon Judah, Jacob was, in effect, saying: "Beginning with the kingdom of Judah, the power to command and rule by the royal line will continue until the coming of Shiloh Messiah, when at that time the royal line of Judah will terminate in Shiloh as the permanent heir.

Since Jewish antiquity, the prophecy of Shiloh meant the Messiah. Thus the Targum of Onkelos renders the verse: 'until the Messiah come, whose is the kingdom.' The Jerusalem Targum renders it: 'until the time that the king Messiah shall come, whose is the kingdom.'

In another account we see clearly how the Most High would ensure that this royal line would continue until Messiah. Judah selected Tamar as a wife for his firstborn Er. But on account of his badness, Er was executed by the Most High. Judah then instructed his second son, Onan, to perform brother-in-law marriage. But Onan "wasted his semen on the earth so as not to give offspring to his brother." For this the Most High also put him to death. The third son Shelah was left, but Judah held back from giving him to Tamar.

Tamar, on learning that her father-in-law was going to Timnah, disguised herself as a prostitute and then seated herself at the entrance of Enaim on the road Judah would be travelling on. Assuming her to be a prostitute, Judah had relations with her, not recognizing she was his daughter-in-law. When Tamar later became pregnant, Judah demanded that she be burned as a harlot. But when Tamar presented the evidence that he himself had made her pregnant, Judah exclaimed: "She is more righteous than I am, for the reason that I did not give her to Shelah my son." **Thus, Tamar had preserved the bloodline of the promised Seed that was to come.** Some six months later Tamar gave birth to the twins Perez and Zerah, as Genesis 38: 25 -30 says:

> "When she was brought out, she sent to her father-in-law, saying, "By the man to whom these belong, I am with child." And she said, "Please determine whose these are—the signet

and cord, and staff." So Judah acknowledged them and said, "She has been more righteous than I, because I did not give her to Shelah my son." And he never had relations with her again. Now it came to pass, at the time for giving birth, that behold, twins were in her womb. And so it was, when she was giving birth, that the one put out his hand; and the midwife took a scarlet thread and bound it on his hand, saying, "This one came out first." Then it happened, as he drew back his hand, that his brother came out unexpectedly; and she said, "How did you break through? This breach be upon you!" Therefore his name was called Perez. Afterward his brother came out who had the scarlet thread on his hand. And his name was called Zerah."

Perez (Rupture; Perineal Rupture), was one of the twin sons of Judah by his daughter-in-law Tamar. At birth, Perez' brother Zerah started to emerge first but withdrew, and Perez came out first, producing a perineal rupture of Tamar (Genesis 38:24-30). Perez retained priority over his brother and is always listed ahead of him, and his house became the more famous of the two (Ruth 4:12). Perez and his own two sons, Hezron and Hamul, are listed among those of Jacob's lineage coming into Egypt, where all three became heads of individual families in Judah (Genesis 46:8,12). Many sons of Perez returned from the Babylonian exile, and 468 of them resided in Jerusalem. (1 Chronicles 9:3,4; Nehemiah 11:4,6)

Jacob and his twelve sons remained living in Egypt. As the sons found wives and their families and grandchildren grew, there soon would be hard times ahead, as Exodus, Chapter One said:

"Then a new king, to whom Joseph meant nothing, came to power in Egypt. ⁹ "Look," he said to his people, "the Israelites have become far too numerous for us. ¹⁰ Come, we must deal shrewdly with them or they will become even more numerous and, if war breaks out, will join our enemies, fight against us and leave the country."

¹¹ So they put slave masters over them to oppress them with forced labor, and they built Pithom and Rameses as store cities for Pharaoh. ¹² But the more they were oppressed, the more they multiplied and spread; so the Egyptians came to dread the Israelites ¹³ and worked them ruthlessly. ¹⁴ They made their lives bitter with harsh slavery in brick and mortar and with every form of slavery in the fields; yes, every form of slavery of theirs the Egyptians worked them ruthlessly."

One manuscript known as *Papyrus Harris I* records Ramses III claiming to have captured innumerable foreign slaves:

"I brought back in great numbers those that my sword has spared, with their hands tied behind their backs before my horses, and their wives and children in tens of thousands, and their livestock in hundreds of thousands. I imprisoned their leaders in fortresses bearing my name, and I added to them chief archers and tribal chiefs, branded and enslaved, tattooed with my name, their wives and children being treated in the same way."

But, would the Seed of Judah remain protected during the harsh slavery of the Pharoah of Egypt? Yes. The Most High used the **Midwives** to preserve the Seed of Judah. Yes, the women Shiphrah and Puah, and the rest of the midwives were courageous sisters. Exodus, Chapter One continues:

"The king of Egypt said to the Hebrew midwives, whose names were Shiphrah and Puah, [16] "When you are helping the Hebrew women during childbirth on the delivery stool, if you see that the baby is a boy, kill him; but if it is a girl, let her live." [17] The midwives, however, feared God and did not do what the king of Egypt had told them to do; they let the boys live. [18] Then the king of Egypt summoned the midwives and asked them, "Why have you done this? Why have you let the boys live?"

> [19] The midwives answered Pharaoh, "Hebrew women are not like Egyptian women; they are vigorous and give birth before the midwives arrive."
>
> [20] So God was kind to the midwives and the people increased and became even more numerous. [21] And because the midwives feared God, he gave them families of their own.
>
> [22] Then Pharaoh gave this order to all his people: "Every Hebrew boy that is born you must throw into the Nile, but let every girl live."

Who were the Judean family members during the many years of Egyptian slavery?
One family member was Hezron. Hezron was the son of Perez and family head of the Judean "Hezronites"; ancestor of King David. At the age of 60, Hezron took the daughter of Machir as wife and by her became father to Segub. His sons Jerahmeel, Ram, and Chelubai (Caleb) apparently were born earlier. Hezron is listed among the 70 "souls of the house of Jacob who came into Egypt."

Another family member was Ram, a descendant of Judah through Perez and Hezron, who lived while Israel was in Egypt. Though Ram was apparently not the first son of Hezron, Ram's genealogy, leading to the Davidic line, is listed first among the three sons of Hezron. His name is spelled Arni (Aram in some manuscripts) in the Book of Luke.

Am·min′a·dab (My People Are Willing (Noble; Generous), another member of the tribe of Judah in Egypt, was a son of Ram of the family of Hezron, tribe of Judah. Amminadab was an ancestor of King David.

Nahshon (from a root meaning "serpent") was a wilderness chieftain of the tribe of Judah. **Nahshon was the son of Amminadab** and among the fifth-listed generation after Judah. Nahshon formed a link in the line of descent that led to David, becoming father to Salmon, who married Rahab, and grandfather of Boaz, who, in turn, married Ruth.

As chieftain of Judah, the leading tribe of Israel, Nahshon assisted Moses with the first wilderness registration of fighting men. He presented a contribution to the tabernacle service when the altar was inaugurated, and he headed Judah's army of 74,600 that led Israel's line of march. Nahshon and Moses were of the same generation. Moses was born in 1593 BCE. **Nahshon's sister Elisheba was the wife of Moses' brother Aaron** (Exodus 6:23). Who was the Pharaoh at the time of Moses' birth?

New archaeological evidence, according to the *Jerusalem Post* and published *in The Journal of Egyptian Archaeology*, reports that slaves were forcibly branded in ancient Egypt to show they were the property of the Pharaoh. Not only were they depicted as property, but they were branded in order to show their status was as low as cattle in ancient society. A series of small branding irons were uncovered that were seen as too small for livestock, and so believed to be used on humans. This collection of 10 branding irons, dates from around 1292 BCE to 656 BCE, during the 19th to 25th dynasties.

The Egyptian kings during the 16th Dynasty may have been the pharaohs during the time of Moses' birth and of his family. One king was Seuserenre Bebiankh, who ruled from 1603 to 1591, or 1600 – 1588 BCE. He left more traces of building projects and mining activity in his reign than most kings of this dynasty. Another Egyptian king was Sewadjenre Nebiryraw I, who reigned from 1627 to 1601 BCE. These kings were ruling during the time of Moses and Nahshon's births and in the lifetime of their families. Whoever was the Pharaoh during Moses' birth and childhood, his name is not recorded in scripture. There is no doubt that Moses knew the name of that Pharaoh, but Moses chose to leave the Pharaoh's name out of the scriptures. Apparently, Pharaoh's name was not important. Why? The reason may lie within Exodus 5:2:

"But Pharaoh said: who is Yehovah so that I should obey his voice to send Israel away? I do not know Yehovah at all."

How did the Most High respond? If Pharaoh did not feel the need to dignify and respect the name of the Most High, then neither would He of Pharaoh. In fact, Yehovah said to Pharaoh:

"For by now I could have thrust my hand out to strike you and your people with a devasting plague…**to have my name declared in all the earth**." (Exodus 9:15,16)

So the Most High Yehovah used the Midwives to preserve the line of Judah, namely Ram, Amminadab, and Nahshon, when they were infants during the time of slavery. The line would continue.

Salmon was the son of Judah's chieftain Nahshon, and likely born during the 40-year wilderness trek. Salmon married Rahab of Jericho. He too, was a link in the genealogical line leading to King David. However, this descendant of Ram, Salmon, whose progeny lived in Bethlehem, should not be confused with the Salma mentioned in 1 Chronicles 2:51,54 as "the father" or builder of Bethlehem, for the latter was a descendant of Ram's brother Caleb.

Boaz was a landowner of Bethlehem in Judah of about the 14th century B.C.E. **Boaz was the son of Salmon (Salma) and Rahab, and was the father of Obed.** He was a link in the family line of the Messiah, the seventh in line of descent from Judah. **Obed had Jesse, and Jesse was the father of David, the King of Judah.**

We will examine more about the royal line of David again later. But now, let us go back to Eden, to a time before the rebellion took place.

CHAPTER 3

The River of Eden

Just prior to the revealing of the first prophecy to mankind, the writer Moses makes mention of another puzzling observation in the garden:

> *"there was a river flowing out of Eden to water the garden, and from there it divided into four rivers."*

In the book of *Berethith*, Moses continues, stating that the river flowing out of Eden split into four rivers:

> *"The name of the first river is Pishon, encircling the entire land of Havilah where there is gold… The name of the second river is Gihon, encircling the entire land of Cush. The name of the third river is Hiddekel, going to the east of Assyria. And the fourth river is the Euphrates."*

The Hiddekel river, known in Persian as the *Tigra*, or in Greek as the *Tigris*, and the Euphrates, both have there source in Eastern Turkey. Modern researchers have yet to identify the first two rivers mentioned, the Pishon and Gihon, although several have presented possibilities.

Ancient historian Herodotus believed the Pishon was the Ganges river in India and that the Gihon was the Nile river. The source of the Ganges comes from the Bhagirathi river off the glaciers in northern India, quite a distance away from the Mesopotamian region. The

Gihon (Giyon) river is recorded on cartographic maps of East Africa, and has been long identified by Ethiopia with the Blue Nile, due to the fact that it encircles the former kingdom of Gojjam. Also contributing to this belief is that the ancient name for Ethiopia was Cush. The source of the Blue Nile is Lake Tana, the largest lake in Ethiopia. Located in Amhara region in the north-western Ethiopian Highlands, Lake Tana is fed by the Gilgey Abay, Reb, and Gumara rivers. The Blue Nile then heads northwest into Sudan, then joins the White Nile, as both tributaries join together and flows through Egypt to the Mediterranean Sea. So now what about the other two rivers that Moses mentioned?

The Tigris, or Hiddekel has its source from the Taurus Mountains in Turkey, south of Lake Hazar about 15 miles (25 km) SE of the city of Elazig. The river emerges from the mountains onto the upper part of the Mesopotamian plain. The Euphrates has two sources. One is at Kara Su, in the SE corner of the Black Sea. The other source is Murat Nehri, originating between Lake Van and Mount Ararat in the Armenian highlands. Here inlays the clue: *The Tigris is just a few miles from one of the sources of the Euphrates River.* This being the case, it is highly probable these two rivers had a *single source* at one time thousands of years ago. This is the strongest evidence to date that suggests the actual location of the Garden of Eden.

We recall that Moses spoke of *the entire land of Cush* which was encircled by a river called Gihon. Ham had a son named Cush. So Ham and his family lived for a time, it appears, by the Black Sea in the Armenian highlands, according to what the Most High inspired to be written down, that the Ark rested on the mountains of Ararat. **But, was Moses perhaps referring instead to the Nubian Ethiopic Kingdom of "Kush" that rose to power in world history?** The Kingdom of Kush emerged as a dominant force beginning around 780 BCE to 350 CE, and becoming Egypt's 25th Dynasty. **However,**

Moses wrote his account about a Land of Cush in 1513 BCE. This was well over *700 years prior* to "Kush" rising to power and sitting on the throne of Pharoah in Egypt.

Therefore, **Moses was referring to an** *earlier Land of Cush* that was either still in existence in his day, or its history passed down orally from the older Jews who were still alive during the time Moses recorded his words. The older generation Hebrews, held as slaves for decades under Pharaoh, knew the story about the Land of Cush. Moses may have also consulted written records about the existence of this earlier Cush. No doubt the source of that information would have come from an eyewitness – Seth – who was there along with his parents Adam and Eve, and passed the knowledge to his sons and grandsons until it reached Noah. In turn, after the flood, Noah passed the account to Shem, Ham, and Japheth, until finally reaching Moses. Even Adam himself may have also shared his eyewitness accounts, since he lived 930 years and saw at least eight generations of his descendants, his own life span overlapping Lamech, Noah's father.

Note something else pertaining to the name Cush. A clay tablet dating to around 3100 – 2900 BCE and discovered in ancient Shinar or Sumer city of Uruk (ancient Erech) contained a seal bearing the name *Kushim,* (a temple administrator recording a business transaction). What is note-worthy about this clay tablet is that it is considered not only the "world's first signature" on an archaeological finding, but the fact there was a person named Kushim dating that far back in time, whose name is so similar to Hamitic *Cush*. (See Notes) If the date of the tablet is correct, this would put the administrator Kushim as a person who lived in the pre-flood world, a contemporary of Adam and Seth. Either way, it is notable to discover such a rare find in the city of Erech (modern Uruk) in the region of ancient Shinar/Sumer, the place where the biblical Cush, son of Ham, son of Noah, was born after the Flood. Following the Flood, Cush's son Nimrod established his kingdom Babel. According to Genesis 10:10:

> "And the beginning of his kingdom was Babel, and Erech, and Accad, and Calneh, in the land of Shinar."

Today there is a village on the eastern coast of the Black Sea in the South Caucasus called Abkhazia, **at a settlement called Adzyubzha, that may hold knowledge to the mysterious 'Land of Cush' story. The people in this village are called** *the Abkhazians of African descent.*

The Abkhazians of African descent were presented in the Russian magazine *Argus* in 1913, which said the existence of African descent people in Russia is a fact, and should "become scientific study" for all to know. Russian scientist P. Kovalevsky wrote that it was most surprising and even a strange fact there was a "whole village" inhabited by "Negroes." Linguist and ethnographer, Dmitri Gulia according to his book *The History of Abkhazia* stated there are similar geographical names of villages, towns, and rivers between Abkhazia and Abyssino – Egyptian regions. (See Notes) The Russian writer Maxim Gorky visited Adzyubzha in 1927 and met some of the elderly Africans. Gorky came to the opinion that the inhabitants in the Caucasus African village were probably descendants from Ethiopia. Perhaps. **However, with all due respect – who is not to say the Ethiopians were instead descendants of an ancient African kingdom** *from the Caucasus*. This is not far-fetched. Ancient Africa was suzerainty to the Palestine region for centuries.

The people in Abkhazia have a folk legend: 'There was a slave ship that wrecked during a great storm along the Black Sea, and the slaves that survived were later sold in the area. The descendants of those sold survivors later founded a colony in Abkhazia.' However, there are two lingering questions about that folk story, which have never yet been answered – how did a ship ever enter the waters of the Black Sea, when the major shipping lanes of the slave trade were conducted far elsewhere? Possibly. But when in history did this great storm occur? Was this folk story alluding to the legend of the global flood?

Another question even more thought-provoking: Does this ancient folk tale establish the possibility that there was once a land in the continent we call *Africa*, **but whose borders once encompassed an area that was in the region of the Black Sea?** This entire discussion on the Abkhazians of African descent does lend weight to possible evidence of a "Land of Cush" near the Tigris and Euphrates Rivers in early human history, within the area of modern-day Armenia and Turkey. The possibility taps our imagination, and opens our minds to a totally different geographical map of the ancient world, in contrast to the taught history we know today. In his book *The Destruction of Black Civilization*, Chancellor Williams stated, for example how ancient China and the Far East, must be a special area of African research. He also asked how do we explain such a large population of Blacks in Southern China, powerful enough to form a kingdom of their own? Or the black people of Formosa, Australia, the Malay peninsula, Indo-China, the Andaman and numerous other islands, as well as the heavy concentration of Africans in India are still open fields for investigation.

Williams then concludes his point by saying this: "All of this will call for a new kind of scholarship, a scholarship without any mission other than the discovery of truth, and one that will not tremble with fear when that truth is contrary to what one prefers to believe."

Consider also the following.

In a research project, the *European Journal of Human Genetics*, volume 24, published a study in 2015 entitled "*Genetic evidence for an origin of the Armenians from Bronze Age mixing of multiple populations.*" The Armenians are a people who have lived for millenniums near the Armenian Highlands, the area where Noah's Ark was said to have rested in scripture. While testing for Armenian genetic mixture relationship to worldwide populations, the study showed that the oldest mixture events appeared to be between populations **related to** *sub-Saharan Africans and West Europeans*, and which occurred around 3800 BCE.

In relation to that, Chancellor Williams said this:

"These are the Blacks who have so puzzled Western scholars that some theorize that *Asia, or Europe may be the homeland of Africans after all.*"

(See Notes)

Let us not forget what the Most High had Moses write down:

"The ark rested on the *mountains of Ararat.*"

Noah had three sons: Ham, Shem, *and Japheth*. As was discussed in the previous chapter, all three sons survived the global flood that wiped away all of disobedient humankind. Ham, Shem, and Japheth survived because they all had the blessing of the Most High Yehovah. Noah's family all shared the same DNA. This is a scientific fact.

We may never know everything about the river that flowed out of Eden, nor of the four rivers that split from it, nor of the exact location of the area called the *Land of Cush*. The Most High will reveal more if He chooses to.

Let us now turn our attention to biblical and historical references to African and Arab Hebrews, and African Jews and Israelites.

CHAPTER 4

Biblical & Historical References to African Jews & Israelites

Zephaniah, whose name means "Jehovah Has Concealed" or "Treasured Up", was a prophet of Yehovah in Judah during King Josiah's reign (659-629) BCE. The Book of Zephaniah contains outstanding prophecies. The foretold destruction upon the Assyrian capital Nineveh and upon Judah and Jerusalem in 607 BCE came true. And the Ammonites, Moabites, and Philistines eventually ceased to exist as a people (Zephaniah 2:4-11). He warned a future day would come when money will have no value in Yehovah's day of Judgment:

> "Neither their silver nor their gold will be able to save them in the day of Jehovah's fury; For by the fire of his zeal the whole earth will be consumed, Because he will make an extermination, indeed a terrible one, of all the inhabitants of the earth." (Zeph 1:18)

Zephaniah may have heard the news reports of such an event, as he had foretold that the great city Nineveh would be destroyed, as did happen in his lifetime (Zeph 2:13-15).

But one of the most fascinating facts that we also learn about the prophet Zephaniah is that he was of African descent. His father's name was *Cushi*, which means "Cushite, Ethiopian."

According to Strong's Concordance, the name Cushi comes from the name *Cush*, which definition is given as "Cush, or Ethiopia, the name of a son of Ham, and of his territory; Also of an Israelite." Strong's Concordance goes on the say – "Cushi, the name of two Israelites; the same as #3569, "Kuwshiy," a Cushite, or descendant of Cush."

We do not know the name of Zephaniah's mother. Not much more is known about his father Cushi, except that Cushi's father was Gedaliah (which means Jehovah Is Great). This Gedaliah is not to be confused with one of the princes in Jerusalem who urged that prophet Jeremiah be put to death, but instead Jeremiah was thrown into a miry cistern. Nor should Cushi's father Gedaliah be confused with Governor Gedaliah, whom King Nebuchadnezzar appointed as governor over the Jews who had been left remaining in the land of Judah, and who was later assassinated by men recruited by the king of Ammon.

Cushi's grandfather was Amariah, who was the son of Hezekiah. More than likely, this Hezekiah was King Hezekiah the king of Judah. There are only three persons with the name Hezekiah in the Hebrew scriptures: King Hezekiah; Hezekiah the grandfather of Cushi (and great-grandfather of Zephaniah); and a man of Israel whose descendants returned with Zerubbabel from the Babylonian exile, mentioned in the book of Ezra.

However, notice how Zephaniah is introduced in the scriptures:

"The word of Jehovah that came to Zeph·a·ni′ah son of Cush′i son of Ged·a·li′ah son of Am·a·ri′ah son of Hez·e·ki′ah in the days of Jo·si′ah son of A′mon the king of Judah."

The fact that Zephaniah is so well introduced into the Hebrew record – citing four generations of his family ancestors, which is unusual – tells us that the Hezekiah mentioned in the record is special – and very likely the king of Judah.

Hezekiah, whose name means "Yehovah Strengthens," was King of Judah from 745-717 BCE. From the beginning of his reign he displayed his zeal for true worship in all Israel.

Assyrian Sennacherib was determined to attack Jerusalem. While Sennacherib and his army began the assault on the Judean city of Lachish, he sent Rabshakeh to demand surrender. He loudly ridiculed Hezekiah and taunted the Most High Jehovah, boasting that Jehovah could no more deliver Jerusalem than the gods of the other nations who were taken over by Assyria. We will continue this discussion of the siege of Lachish later in Chapter 9.

Around the time of Sennacherib's threats against Jerusalem, Hezekiah was afflicted with a malignant boil. At that time Hezekiah did not as yet have a son. It appeared that the royal line of David was in danger of dying out, as well as the promised Seed of Judah that was to come. Hezekiah prayed to Yehovah, who sent Isaiah to inform Hezekiah that he would have 15 years added to his life. A miraculous sign was given, the shadow of the sun would move back ten steps on "the stairs of Ahaz." In the third year after that, Hezekiah had a son named Manasseh, who later succeeded him on the throne at the age of 12. Manasseh's mother was Hephzibah.

At some point, either by Hephzibah or by some other wife or concubine, Hezekiah had another son called Amariah – the grandfather of Cushi.

Gedaliah's wife is unknown. Was she Hamitic? Or, was Gedaliah? For some reason, Gedaliah's son was named Cushi. There is only one reasonable explanation. The child's ancestry pointed to a descendant of Cush.

There is also another person named Cushi. He too, is of African descent.

Je·hudi, whose name means *A Jew; (Belonging to) Judah*, was an officer of King Jehoiakim of Judah, son of King Josiah. He was sent by the princes of Judah to bring to them Baruch with Jeremiah's scroll. When Jehudi read the scroll to Jehoiakim, the king cut it up and burned it, throwing it into the brazier:

> "The king was sitting in the winter house, in the ninth month, with a fire burning in the brazier before him. After Je·hu′di had read three or four columns, the king would cut off that portion with the secretary's knife and pitch it into the fire that was burning in the brazier, until the entire scroll ended up in the fire that was in the brazier."

Interestingly, the Hebrew word rendered "brazier (*'ach*) is of Egyptian origin. This suggests that the brazier was an innovation from Egypt. King Jehoiakim had a brazier in his winter house.

Jehudi's father was Nethaniah (Jehovah Has Given), his grandfather was Shelemiah (Jehovah is Recompense), and Jehudi's great-grandfather was Cushi, a natural-born Jew. His name and that of his ancestor are thought by some to denote that he was not a Jew by birth, but a proselyte, but there is no evidence supporting that view. And, as has already been stated, the name Cushi means "Cushite, Ethiopian." Jehudi's great-grandfather was a descendant of Cush, and born in Israel.

We know that Jacob had 12 sons. One of them, Joseph, was sold into slavery by his jealous brothers, and Joseph was made a slave in Egypt. But the Most High was controlling matters for Joseph and all of his father Jacob's family, who were to preserve the promised Seed that was promised to come.

During that time in Egypt, Joseph's wife Asenath bore him two sons, Manasseh and Ephraim. What is often overlooked is that Asenath was Egyptian, the daughter of Potiphera of Egypt.

We know later at Jacob's deathbed that the two sons Ephraim and Manasseh, part Hamitic, would later form two tribes to make up the 12 tribes of Israel. We will discuss this soon. But let us fast forward to when the Israelites left Egypt during the Exodus and examine the successor of Moses, who was Joshua.

Josh′u·a (shortened form of Jehoshua, meaning "Jehovah Is Salvation") was one of the 12 spies sent by Moses to spy out the Promised Land in 1512 BCE. Joshua, the Son of Nun, was an *Ephraimite*. So Joshua was also part Hamitic. Joshua was a bold and fearless leader, and obedient to divine direction. So Moses sent out the 12 men to spy out the Promised Land. Forty days later only Joshua and Caleb brought back a good report. But the ten spies brought back a bad report.

For the ten spies' lack of faith, Yehovah sentenced the Israelites to wander in the wilderness for 40 years until all the registered males from 20 years old upward died off. Of the registered adult males, Joshua and Caleb were the only ones that would enter the Promised Land in 1473 BCE (and the Levites, who were not registered among the other Israelites for military duty):

Numbers 14: 29-31

> "Your dead bodies shall fall in this wilderness, and of all your number, listed in the census from twenty years old and upward, who have grumbled against me, [30] not one shall come into the land where I swore that I would make you dwell, except Caleb the son of Jephunneh and Joshua the

son of Nun. [31] But your little ones, who you said would become a prey,I will bring in, and they shall know the land that you have rejected."

At the age of 110 years, Joshua died and was buried at Timnath-serah. A census was taken of Israel's tribes while they were in the wilderness:

Numbers 26: 28-37
"**The sons of Joseph by their families were: Ma·nas′seh and E′phra·im.** The sons of Ma·nas′seh were: of Ma′chir, the family of the Ma′chir·ites; and Ma′chir became father to Gil′e·ad; of Gil′e·ad, the family of the Gil′e·ad·ites. These were the sons of Gil′e·ad: of Ie′zer, the family of the Ie′zer·ites; of He′lek, the family of the He′lek·ites; of As′ri·el, the family of the As′ri·el·ites; of She′chem, the family of the She′chem·ites; of She·mi′da, the family of the She·mi′da·ites; of He′pher, the family of the He′pher·ites. Now Ze·lo′phe·had the son of He′pher had no sons, only daughters, and the names of the daughters of Ze·lo′phe·had were Mah′lah, Noah, Hog′lah, Mil′cah, and Tir′zah. These were the families of Ma·nas′seh, and their registered ones were 52,700. These were the sons of E′phra·im by their families: of Shu′the·lah, the family of the Shu′thel·a′hites; of Be′cher, the family of the Be′cher·ites; of Ta′han, the family of the Ta′han·ites. And these were the sons of Shu′the·lah: of E′ran, the family of the E′ran·ites. These were the families of the sons of E′phra·im, and their registered ones were 32,500. These were the sons of Joseph by their families."

Eventually, the 12 tribes came out of the wilderness and began to enter Canaan, the promised land. All the adult males, who had been over twenty years of age on that day of Yehovah's sentence, died off, including those in the tribes of Ephraim and Manessah, except for Joshua, Caleb, and the Levites. However, the males of the 12 Tribes who had been under twenty years and the females were allowed to enter Canaan. This included the children and women of Ephraim and Mannaseh:

Joshua 5: 2-7

"At that time the Lord said unto Joshua, Make thee sharp knives, and circumcise again the children of Israel the second time.

And Joshua made him sharp knives, and circumcised the children of Israel at the hill of the foreskins.

And this is the cause why Joshua did circumcise: All the people that came out of Egypt, that were males, even all the men of war, died in the wilderness by the way, after they came out of Egypt.

All the people who left Egypt were circumcised, but all the people born in the wilderness on the journey after they left Egypt were not circumcised. The Israelites had walked for 40 years in the wilderness until the entire nation had died off, that is, the men of war who left Egypt who did not obey the voice of Jehovah. Jehovah swore to them that he would never let them see the land that Jehovah had sworn to their forefathers to give to us, a land flowing with milk and honey.

And their children, whom he raised up in their stead, them Joshua circumcised: for they were uncircumcised, because they had not circumcised them by the way."

Another census was taken after the Israelites reached Canaan. Here were the survivors of Ephraim and Manessah after they reached the Promised Land:

I Chronicles 7: 14-27

The sons of Manasseh; Ashriel, whom she bare: (but his concubine the Aramitess bare Machir the father of Gilead:

> [15] And Machir took to wife the sister of Huppim and Shuppim, whose sister's name was Maachah;) and the name of the second was Zelophehad: and Zelophehad had daughters.

> [16] And Maachah the wife of Machir bare a son, and she called his name Peresh; and the name of his brother was Sheresh; and his sons were Ulam and Rakem.

> [17] And the sons of Ulam; Bedan. These were the sons of Gilead, the son of Machir, the son of Manasseh.

> [18] And his sister Hammoleketh bare Ishod, and Abiezer, and Mahalah.

> [19] And the sons of Shemidah were, Ahian, and Shechem, and Likhi, and Aniam.

> [20] And the sons of Ephraim; Shuthelah, and Bered his son, and Tahath his son, and Eladah his son, and Tahath his son,

> [21] And Zabad his son, and Shuthelah his son, and Ezer, and Elead, whom the men of Gath that were born in that land slew, because they came down to take away their cattle.

> [22] And Ephraim their father mourned many days, and his brethren came to comfort him.

> [23] And when he went in to his wife, she conceived, and bare a son, and he called his name Beriah, because it went evil with his house.

²⁴ (And his daughter was Sheerah, who built Bethhoron the nether, and the upper, and Uzzensherah.)

²⁵ And Rephah was his son, also Resheph, and Telah his son, and Tahan his son.

²⁶ Laadan his son, Ammihud his son, Elishama his son.

²⁷ Non his son, Jehoshuah his son.

Notice the close relationship conveyed, as expressed in Psalm 77:15:

> "With your power you have rescued your people, The sons of Jacob **and of Joseph.** (*Selah*)"

We will highlight the daughters of Zelophehad and also the woman named Sheerah in Chapter 8.

Another nugget of truth: In examining the genealogy of Yeshua's parents, Joseph and Mary in the biblical books of Matthew and Luke, we find that they both were descendants of the line of Judah by means of King David. Matthew's genealogical listing shows Joseph a descendant through David's son Solomon. Luke's genealogical record shows Mary a descendant through David's son Nathan. What is even more interesting is that after the two genealogical lines diverge at Solomon and Nathan, both lines come together again in two persons, Shealtiel and Zerubbabel.

1 Chronicles 3: 1 – 9, 17-19.

"These were the sons of David who were born to him in Heb'ron: the firstborn Am'non, whose mother was A·hin'o·am of Jez're·el; the second, Daniel, whose mother was Ab'i·gail the Car'mel·ite; ² the third, Ab'sa·lom the son of Ma'a·cah the daughter of Tal'mai the king of Gesh′ur; the fourth, Ad·o·ni′jah the son of Hag′gith; ³ the fifth, Sheph·a·ti′ah, whose mother was A·bi′tal; and the sixth, Ith′re·am, whose mother was David's wife Eg′lah. ⁴ These six were born to him in Heb′ron; he reigned there for 7 years and 6 months, and for 33 years he reigned in Jerusalem. ⁵ These were born to him in Jerusalem: Shim′e·a, Sho′bab, Nathan, and Sol′o·mon; the mother of these four was Bath-she′ba the daughter of Am′mi·el. ⁶ And nine other sons were Ib′har, E·lish′a·ma, E·liph′e·let, ⁷ No′gah, Ne′pheg, Ja·phi′a, ⁸ E·lish′a·ma, E·li′a·da, and E·liph′e·let. ⁹ All of these were the sons of David, besides the sons of the concubines, and Ta′mar was their sister.

> "**The sons of Jec·o·ni′ah the prisoner were She·al′ti·el,** Mal·chi′ram, **Pe·dai′ah,** She·naz′zar, Jek·a·mi′ah, Hosh′a·ma, and Ned·a·bi′ah. **The sons of Pe·dai′ah were Ze·rub′ba·bel** and Shim′e·i; and the sons of Ze·rub′ba·bel were Me·shul′lam and Han·a·ni′ah (and She·lo′mith was their sister)."

"After the deportation to Babylon, Jec·o·ni′ah became father to She·al′ti·el; She·al′ti·el became father to Ze·rub′ba·bel. (Matthew 1:12)

Ze·rub′ba·bel,e
son of She·al′ti·el,d
son of Ne′ri," (Luke 3:27)

Pedaiah, the son of Jeconiah, was born during the Babylonian exile and became father to Governor Zerubbabel, in the link leading to Yeshua. However, due to some unexplained circumstance, Zerubbabel is also called the son of Pedaiah's brother Shealtiel. How can this be? Shealtiel may have adopted Zerubbabel if Pedaiah died.

Or, if Shealtiel died before fathering a son, Pedaiah may have performed brother-in-law marriage with Shealtiel's wife, who gave birth to Zerubbabel, but naming his brother Shealtiel as the father in honor to him. (Ezra 5:2; Matthew 1:12)

Another explanation could be that since Shealtiel was the son of Jeconiah perhaps by marriage to the daughter of Neri he became Neri's son-in-law, so could be called the "son of Neri." (**Matt 1:12; Luke 3:27**)

We should also note too, that according to the genealogical line of Mary's husband Joseph, the carpenter in Nazareth, would make the Hamitic Asenath an ancestral forebear to Joseph and his children, including his two sons James and Jude, who were writers of two books in the Greek scriptures, also called the New Testament.

Let us now examine historical evidence of Jews and Israelites in ancient North and East Africa.

A Jewish presence in Egypt was attested at least as early as the sixth century BCE. During that period, Jeremiah directed a message to Jews living in various localities of Egypt, including Memphis. As Jeremiah 44:1,2 says:

"The word that came to Jeremiah concerning *all the Jews which dwell in the land of Egypt*, which dwell at Migdol, and at Tahpanhes, and at Noph, and in the country of Pathros, saying, "Thus saith Jehovah of armies, the God of Israel; Ye have seen all the evil that I have brought upon Jerusalem, and upon all the cities of Judah; and, behold, this day they are a desolation, and no man dwelleth therein."

Egypt supported Babylon against the rising power of Medo-Persia. But by 525 B.C.E., the land was subjugated by Cambyses II, son of Cyrus the Great, and thereby came under Persian imperial rule. While many Jews doubtless left Egypt to return to their homeland, others remained in Egypt. Thus, there was a Jewish colony in

Elephantine (Egyptian, *Yeb*), an island in the Nile near Aswan, south of Cairo. A valuable archaeological find in the colony of Elephantine is thousands of documents dating to the 5th century BCE. which reveals conditions prevailing there during about the same time as when Ezra and Nehemiah were active in Jerusalem. These documents, in Aramaic, contain the name of Sanballat of Samaria (Nehemiah 4:1,2) and of Johanan the high priest. (Nehemiah 12:22) Of interest is an official order issued during the reign of Darius II (423-405 BCE) that "the festival of unfermented cakes" be celebrated by the colony.

It is widely agreed that this Elephantine community originated in the mid-seventh or mid-sixth centuries BCE, likely as a result of Judean and Samaritan refugees fleeing into Egypt during the times of Assyrian and Babylonian invasions.

The papyri also documents' the existence of a small Jewish temple at Elephantine, which possessed altars for incense offerings and animal sacrifices, as late as 411 BCE. Such a temple would be in clear violation of the law, which stipulates that no Jewish temple may be constructed outside of Jerusalem.

Another account in recorded history is the time during the 5th Century BCE when a proclamation was decreed to kill and destroy all Jews in Ethiopia and Egypt, as well as any other Persian district where Jews were residing. This was during the Persian Empire under King Ahasuerus, also known as Xerxes I. From the Elephantine Papyri is a letter addressed to Bagoas, governor of Judah as a request for the rebuilding of a Jewish temple at Elephantine, which had been destroyed by Egyptian pagans during a rampage of violence. The letter is dated year 17 of King Darius (III). It is unclear whether the attack on the Hebrew temple in Elephantine was triggered by Persian King Ahasuerus' decree or not. However, this archaeological find gives a glimpse into the threats that existed towards the Black Jews in Ethiopia and Egypt.

In the Book of Esther, Chapter Three, it mentions of the attack on the Jews in all the districts of Persia, which included Ethiopia and Egypt:

"Then Haman said to King Xerxes, "There is a certain people dispersed among the peoples in all the provinces of your kingdom who keep themselves separate. Their customs are different from those of all other people, and they do not obey the king's laws; it is not in the king's best interest to tolerate them. If it pleases the king, let a decree be issued to destroy them, and I will give ten thousand talents[a] of silver to the king's administrators for the royal treasury."

So the king took his signet ring from his finger and gave it to Haman son of Hammedatha, the Agagite, the enemy of the Jews. "Keep the money," the king said to Haman, "and do with the people as you please."

Then on the thirteenth day of the first month the royal secretaries were summoned. They wrote out in the script of each province and in the language of each people all Haman's orders to the king's satraps, the governors of the various provinces and the nobles of the various peoples. These were written in the name of King Xerxes himself and sealed with his own ring. Dispatches were sent by couriers to all the king's provinces with the order to destroy, kill and annihilate all the Jews—young and old, women and children—on a single day, the thirteenth day of the twelfth month, the month of Adar, and to plunder their goods."

We notice the decree was sent "to all the king's provinces." Queen Esther exposed Haman as the perpetrator behind the genocidal decree. The King had him executed. Then the king urged Esther and Mordecai to quickly send a decree to somehow foil or curtail the planned attack on the Jews. This would include the Black Jews that resided in Ethiopia and Egypt. Notice what transpired next in Esther 8:9-10:

"Then were the king's scribes called at that time in the third month, that is, the month Sivan, on the three and twentieth day thereof; and it was written according to all that Mordecai commanded unto the Jews, and to the lieutenants, and the deputies and rulers **of the provinces which are from India unto Ethiopia**, a hundred twenty and seven provinces, unto every province according to the writing thereof, **and unto every people after their language, and to the Jews** according to their writing, and according to their language. He wrote it in the name of King A·has·u·e′rus and sealed it with the king's signet ring **and sent the written documents** by the hand of couriers on horses; they rode on swift post-horses, bred for royal service."

Let us examine the account found in the book of Acts 2: 5-12, in regards to the festival of Pentecost that was celebrated every year in Jerusalem. Many Jews from all over the then-known world at that time came to Jerusalem to the festival. This particular account involves the festival that took place in 33 CE:

"And there were dwelling at Jerusalem Jews, devout men, out of every nation under heaven.

⁶ Now when this was noised abroad, the multitude came together, and were confounded, because that every man heard them speak in his own language.

⁷ And they were all amazed and marvelled, saying one to another, Behold, are not all these which speak Galilaeans?

⁸ And how hear we every man in our own tongue, wherein we were born?

⁹ Parthians, and Medes, and Elamites, and the dwellers in Mesopotamia, and in Judaea, and Cappadocia, in Pontus, and Asia,

¹⁰ Phrygia, and Pamphylia, in Egypt, and in the parts of Libya about Cyrene, and strangers of Rome, Jews and proselytes,

¹¹ Cretes and Arabians, we do hear them speak in our tongues the wonderful works of God.

¹² And they were all amazed, and were in doubt, saying one to another, What meaneth this?"

This was written in 33 CE. We notice the scripture said there were Jews not only in Egypt, but also the regions in Libya near Cyrene. Ancient Cyrene today is now an archaeological site in the Libyan village now called Shahhat.

One of the regions in Libya and near Cyrene in biblical days was an ancient city called Sirte, also called Surt and Syrtis.

Sirte was a city located on the Libyan coast between Tripoli and Benghazi and near the Gulf of Sirte, also called the Gulf of Sidra on the Mediterranean. The evidence of the earliest existence of Jews in Libya is found in Sirte, according to archaeological surveys on the Barion or Baryon area, where there was a Jewish synagogue found that dated back to at least the 10th century BCE.

This would take us back to at least the time of Solomon's fleet of ships that sailed to Tarshish in this region with a ship crew of Judeans and Phoenicians. These Judean sailors of Solomon would have the need to keep practicing the requirements of the Most High's law even when on voyages faraway from home. Establishing synagogues at various stops on their sailing journeys would meet that need.

In the Book of Acts 27: 10-17, the Benjamite Saul who later followed Yeshua and became Paul passed by "Syrtis" during the shipwreck when he was being transported as a prisoner:

> "Men, I can see that our voyage is going to be disastrous and bring great loss to ship and cargo, and to our own lives also." But the centurion, instead of listening to what Paul said, followed the advice of the pilot and of the owner of the ship. Since the harbor was unsuitable to winter in, the majority decided that we should sail on, hoping to reach Phoenix and winter there. This was a harbor in Crete, facing both southwest and northwest. When a gentle south wind began to blow, they saw their opportunity; so they weighed anchor and sailed along the shore of Crete. Before very long, a wind of hurricane force, called the Northeaster, swept down from the island. The ship was caught by the storm and could not head into the wind; so we gave way to it and were driven along. As we passed to the lee of a small island called Cauda, we were hardly able to make the lifeboat secure, so the men hoisted it aboard. Then they passed ropes under the ship itself to hold it together. Because they were afraid they would run aground on the sandbars of **Syrtis**, they lowered the sea anchor and let the ship be driven along."

Syrtis, or Sirte, was built about 31 miles (50 km) east of the ancient Phoenician city of Macomedes, today known as the village of As-Sultan. According to a description from Map 37 Syrtica, "the region of Syrtica is one of the least hospitable coastal stretches anywhere in the Mediterranean basin...on the eastern side of the gulf beyond Kozynthion Akron, dispersed ancient settlements increase in number...some of the major sites were known in the latter sources by their Greek names and in the former by the Latin/Phoenician/Libyan equivalents...the majority of the settlement names current in the Roman period were of Libyan or Phoenician derivation."

The crew, therefore, feared that the ship would be run aground on the "Syrtis," evidently the quicksands or sandbanks of the Gulf of Sidra.

Notice what historian Philo makes mention in regards to Judean colonies:

The Works of Philo - ON THE EMBASSY TO GAIUS (Written in 38 CE)

"Concerning the holy city I must now say what is necessary. It, as I have already stated, is my native country, and the metropolis, not only of the one country **of Judaea, but also of many, by reason of the colonies which it has sent out from time to time into the bordering districts of Egypt, Phoenicia**, Syria in general, and especially that part of it which is called Coelo-Syria, and also with those more distant regions of Pamphylia, Cilicia, the greater part of Asia Minor as far as Bithynia, and the furthermost corners of Pontus. And in the same manner into Europe, into Thessaly, and Boeotia, and Macedonia, and Aetolia, and Attica, and Argos, and Corinth and all the most fertile and wealthiest districts of Peloponnesus. And not only are the continents full of Jewish colonies, but also all the most celebrated islands are so too; such as Euboea, and Cyprus, and Crete. "I say nothing of the countries beyond the Euphrates, for all of them except a very small portion, and Babylon, and all the satrapies around, which have any advantages whatever of soil or climate, have Jews settled in them. So that if my native land is, as it reasonably may be, looked upon as entitled to a share in your favour, it is not one city only that would then be benefited by you, but ten thousand of them in every region of the habitable world, in Europe, in Asia, **and in Africa**, on the continent, in the islands, on the coasts, and in the inland parts."

Notice what is found in *A Treatise Against Flaccus* (written c. 38 CE):

> "Knowing that the city had two classes of inhabitants, our own nation and the people of the country, and that the whole of Egypt was inhabited in the same manner, and that Jews who inhabited Alexandria and the rest of the country from the Catabathmos on the side of **Libya to the boundaries of Ethiopia** were not less than a million of men."

We recall in Acts 2: 26-34 the disciple Philip was guided by the Spirit to go down to the road that led to Gaza according to the account:

> "Now an angel of the Lord said to Philip, "Go south to the road—the desert road—that goes down from Jerusalem to Gaza." So he started out, and on his way he met an Ethiopian eunuch, an important official in charge of all the treasury of the Kandake (which means "queen of the Ethiopians"). This man had gone to Jerusalem to worship, and on his way home was sitting in his chariot reading the Book of Isaiah the prophet. The Spirit told Philip, "Go to that chariot and stay near it."

Then Philip ran up to the chariot and heard the man reading Isaiah the prophet. "Do you understand what you are reading?" Philip asked.

"How can I," he said, "unless someone explains it to me?" So he invited Philip to come up and sit with him.

This is the passage of Scripture the eunuch was reading:

"He was led like a sheep to the slaughter,
and as a lamb before its shearer is silent,
so he did not open his mouth.
In his humiliation he was deprived of justice.
Who can speak of his descendants?
For his life was taken from the earth."

The eunuch asked Philip, "Tell me, please, who is the prophet talking about, himself or someone else?"

Then Philip began with that very passage of Scripture and told him the good news about Jesus. As they traveled along the road, they came to some water and the eunuch said, "Look, here is water. What can stand in the way of my being baptized?" And he gave orders to stop the chariot. Then both Philip and the eunuch went down into the water and Philip baptized him.

When they came up out of the water, the Spirit of the Lord suddenly took Philip away, and the eunuch did not see him again, but went on his way rejoicing."

This brings up the question: How did Ethiopia come to know about the covenants of the Most High? How did this Ethiopian Jewish government official – which was what the word Eunuch meant in his case – come to have a copy of the Book of Isaiah? And, who was this particular Kandake queen of Ethiopia?

Ethiopia no doubt heard about the Most High during the time of King Solomon's rule. Even the Queen of Sheba in the area near Yemen heard about Solomon and went to Jerusalem to see for herself the Judean Kingdom and to meet Solomon. She returned home praising the God of Solomon. Besides the Kingdom of Sheba, the stories and accounts about Solomon and the Kingdom of Judah without question spread throughout Ethiopia.

Sometime between 1943 BCE and 1932 BCE) a famine forced Abraham to leave Canaan and go down to Egypt.

> "And the princes of Phar'aoh also saw her, and they began praising her to Phar'aoh, so that the woman was taken to the house of Phar'aoh. He treated A'bram well because of her, and he acquired sheep, cattle, male and female donkeys, male and female servants, and camels. Then Jehovah struck Phar'aoh and his household with severe plagues because of Sar'ai, A'bram's wife. So Phar'aoh called A'bram and said: "What is this you have done to me? Why did you not tell me that she was your wife? Why did you say, 'She is my sister,' so that I was about to take her as my wife? Here is your wife. Take her and go!" So Phar'aoh gave his men orders concerning him, and they sent him away with his wife and all that he had." (Genesis 12: 15-20)

Word may have spread to Ethiopia during Abraham's stay in Egypt about the true God whom he worshipped.

Ethiopia may also have known about the Most High when the Northern ten-tribes were taken exile into Cush by the Assyrians in 740 BCE.

Judean exiles were foretold to return to their homeland from Cush and other faraway lands.

> "In that day the Lord will reach out his hand a second time to reclaim the surviving remnant of his people from Assyria,

from Lower Egypt, from Upper Egypt, from Cush, from Elam, from Babylonia, from Hamath and from the islands of the Mediterranean." (Isaiah 11:11)

The Ethiopian official who was reading the Book of Isaiah may have obtained a copy of that Hebrew scroll from the Egyptian city of Alexandria. He may also have received his copy from Ezra. Ezra was known as "a skilled copyist in the law of Moses," indicating that copies of Yehovah's Law had been brought from Judah by the scattered Jewish diaspora in Media, Babylon, Cush, and Persia, which included Cush within its domain at one time.

"Now in the days of A·has·u·e′rus, that is, the A·has·u·e′rus who ruled over 127 provinces from *In′di·a to E·thi·o′pi·a,* in those days when King A·has·u·e′rus was sitting on his royal throne in Shu′shan the citadel, in the third year of his reign, he held a banquet for all his princes and his servants. The army of Persia and Me′di·a, the nobles, and the princes of the provinces were before him." (Esther 1: 1-3)

Additionally, Ethiopia could have learned about the Most High Yehovah when Jacob and his family were invited by Joseph, together with all their livestock and belongings, to move down to the fertile land of Goshen in Egypt, since the great famine at that time was still raging. Pharaoh even provided wagons and food provisions for their move. And Ethiopia yet again no doubt heard the news about how the Most High through Moses brought the ten plagues onto Pharaoh's Egypt and the climatic exodus out of Egypt and crossing of the Red Sea on foot. Surely there were those in Ethiopia who did put their faith in the God of the Israelites when they heard what had happened in Egypt.

Who was the Kandake queen of Kush (Cush, Ethiopia), that the Ethiopian Jew was serving under as official over her treasures? There were several queens and queen regents (wife of a king) who ruled in Kush's history. One of the earliest known was Nahirqo, who ruled in the middle 2nd Century BCE. She is buried in a pyramid at Meroe. Nahirqo's husband was King Adikhalamani. Another queen was that of Kandake Amanirenas. She is known for leading the Kushite army against the Romans and halted Roman expansion into Kush during 25-22 BCE. According to Strabo, she commanded thousands of men. After a Roman victory by Gaius Petronius, the prefect of Egypt, Amanirenas sent ambassadors, who were escorted to Rome, and a peace treaty was established. Kandake Amanirenas' reign ended by the beginning of the 1st Century CE.

According to the Biblical account in 33 CE, the Ethiopian official had gone to Jerusalem to worship, and when returning back to Kush was met by Philip, one of Yeshua's disciples. There are three possible queens who may have been the ruler whom the Ethiopian Jew served under. One of them possibly was Kandake Amanishakheto, the successor of Amanirenas. She was known for her vast treasure of jewelry. Kandake Amanishakheto ruled in the early 1st Century. Her successor was Queen regent Shanakdakhete, who also reigned in the first half of the 1st Century, and therefore could have been the second possibility. The third queen may have been Kandake Amanitore. Some place her reign as beginning in 1 BCE until 50 CE, whereas others say she began her reign in the middle of the 1st Century. Kandake Amanitore, who is buried at Meroe, co-reigned with her son, Natakamani. (See Notes)

Now let us examine several historical references outside the Hebrew Scriptures.

According to historian Josephus, ninety-seven thousand Jews were taken captive in the Jewish - Roman revolt in 70 CE, many of whom were sent as slaves to Egypt. Many of them were probably sent to Egypt in ships, as the Romans had a fleet in the Mediterranean. (See Notes) This was a much quicker way of transporting them instead of by land across the desert. This was in fulfillment of Deuteronomy 28:68:

> "And Jehovah will certainly bring you back to Egypt by ship, by the way that I told you, 'You will never see it again,' and there you will have to sell yourselves to your enemies as male and female slaves, but there will be no buyer."

Later in Chapter 12 will be shown the connection of Deuteronomy 28:68 to the ships mentioned in the Book of Revelation.

Strabo, the Greek historian who lived between 64 BCE to 24 CE, said this about the Jews:

> "The ancestors of the Jews were Egyptians."

Tacitus, a Roman historian in the 1st Century CE, reported this about the ancient Jews:

> "Many say they were a race of Ethiopian origin."

If there is any doubt as to what skin tone the Ethiopians were, one can read the poem written by the Anglo-Saxon poet Caedmon in the 7th Century CE entitled *Exodus*, where he calls the Ethiopians "a race burned brown by the heat of the sun." Again, Tacitus mentioned that the Romans in his day viewed the Jews as "Ethiopian." Of course, Jews were Semitic, and of dark skin. Some were also Hamitic.

There was a map of Africa made by Italian cartographer Livio Sanuto and his brother Giulio Sanuto. Livio died in 1576, and so his brother Giulio published the map in 1588. On the map in the area around the Congo are the words written in Latin: IUDEORUM TERRA. When translated means: "LAND OF THE JEWS."

In 1678-1679, French explorer Jean Barbot wrote in his account that the Jews in Portugal and southern Spain were so dark that European whites thought that all Jews were dark or black.

An atlas entitled *Atlas Geographus, Or A Complete System of Geography, Ancient And Modern*, published during 1711 - 1717, made this comment: Judaism was the Religion of the Ancient Africans for a long time."

Regarded by his contemporaries for producing some of the most detailed and accurate maps of his era, Welsh engraver Emanuel Bowen published a map of Africa in 1747 entitled *Negroland*. On the map in the area around present-day Benin (formerly called Dahomey) in West Africa is engraved "Kingdom of Juda or Whidah SLAVE COAST." French geographer Elisee Reclus also took note of this same Kingdom of Juda in his book *The Earth and Its Inhabitants* in 1888:

> "East of great PoPo begins the Dahomey territory guarded by the important town of Glehweh, known to Europeans by the various names of Fida, Hevedah, Whyda, Wida. The old writers called it Juda, and it's inhabitants were said to be Jews."

Also, in connection with this same Kingdom of Juda in West Africa, the University of Montepellier in France published a geography book in 1890 in French which said this:

> "Whydah (Fida, Hwedah, Ouida, Juda, ou Ajuda) est une ville ancienne, frequentee depuis le xvi siecle par les negriers portugais, qui lui donnerent son nom. Ses habitants etaient dits les Judaiques, et on les considerait en effet comme un reste de tribus dispersees d'Israel."

Translation: Whyah (Fida, Hwedah, Ouida, Juda or Ajuda) is a city old, frequented since the sixteenth century by Portuguese slavers who gave it its name. Its inhabitants were said to be the Judaic and they were indeed considered to be a remnant of scattered tribes of Israel."

Also again, this same region was reported on in 1930, by university professor and historian Allen H. Godbey in his book *The Lost Tribes A Myth*:

> "In the interior of Dahomey...is a large Jewish community... Jewish scholar, Dr. J. Kreppel, reports that they have a central temple, where sacrifices are still offered. Their principal laws are engraved on plaster tablets fastened around the temple walls. They have a Pentateuch written on parchment in Hebrew letters, but they have no other books...their Judaism is a matter of oral traditions. They cling to the Sabbath, and to certain Jewish customs despite the influence of pagan surroundings. There is a high-priest, with many priestly families, whose membership goes about giving moral and religious instruction to the families of the community."

Traveller and author Thomas Edward Bowditch published a map of West Africa in 1819, where at the top portion of the map is engraved a village town called *Yahoodee*. In the book *An Account of Timbuctoo & Housa* published in 1820, makes mention of Yahoodee:

"This place is reported to be inhabited by one of the lost tribes of Israel, possibly an emigration from the tribe of Judah. Yahooda, in African Arabic, signifies Judah. Yahoodee signifies Jew. It is not impossible, that many of the lost tribes of Israel may be found dispersed in the interior regions of Africa."

Another book, written in 1824 by Joseph Dupuis, British Consul to the Ashanti Empire, also mentions of Yahoodee:

"Beginning then at the top of the map, I find a place called Yahoodee, a country or town of non-existence. Yahoodee simply implies Jews, the tribes of Jews, etc. which term the Moslems apply to those people of the Mosaic faith who inhabit the lower Atlas, and the districts of Suse. They also apply the term Yahoodee to the Hebrew or Jewish tribes, whether native Africans or not."

According to *History of the Jews* by Professor H. Graetz, there were Jewish families who had reached Spain, having fled Judea after the Temple had been destroyed in 607 BCE, by the conquest of Babylonian Nebuchadnezzar. Actually, that area would not have been called Spain at that time. Instead, the region would have been Tarshish/Iberia, which was later colonized by Carthage, and then eventually becoming Spain. Graetz mentions certain Jewish families - the Ibn Dauds, the Abrabanels, the Nasi - who maintained that their ancestors were of the line of King David, which the Nasi family were able to prove by means of genealogical documents and seals. Graetz also mentioned other Jewish families in Spain who had fled Judea during the destruction of the second temple in 70 CE. by the Romans.

In connection with Jews in Portugal, French Naturalist and Cosmologist Georges-Louis Leclerc de Buffon said in 1792 "the Jews of Portugal alone are tawny."

British ethnologist James Cowles Prichard said in 1845: "the Jews of Portugal are very dark."

Samuel Stanhope Smith, a minister and president of Princeton, said in the late eighteenth century about the Jews: "They are…brown in France and in Turkey, swarthy in Portugal and Spain…tawny or copper-colored in Arabia and Egypt."

The Duchess d'Abrantes, wife of the ambassador to Portugal in the time of Napoleon said: "the Jew, the Negro and the Portuguese could be seen in a single person."

There are many, many more historical references to the original Jews, Israelites, and Hebrews. However, we will conclude this chapter by sharing one more source:

Eliezer Ben Hurcanus, or Hycanus (80 - 118 CE), is considered one of the most prominent sages of the 1st and 2nd Centuries in Judea. He was a member of the Sanhedrin. Although later excommunicated because he dissented from a decision by the majority Sanhedrin regarding an interpretation of the law, his excommunication was later revoked.

In Jewish rabbinic readings is the midrash work entitled "Pirkei DeRabbi Eliezer" (Chapters of Rabbi Eliezer), which is traditionally ascribed to Hurcanus and was edited in the 8th or 9th century CE. In Chapter 24, entitled *Nimrod And The Tower Of Babel* it says this:

> "Noah brought his sons and his grandsons, and he blessed them with their settlements, and he gave them as an inheritance all the earth. He especially blessed Shem and his sons, dark but comely, and he gave them the habitable earth.

He blessed Ham and his sons, dark like the raven, and he gave them as an inheritance the coast of the sea. He blessed Japheth and his sons, them entirely white, and he gave them for an inheritance the desert and its fields; these which he endowed them."

In later years of his life, Eliezer Ben Hurcanus was quoted as saying "I have never taught anything which I had not learned from my masters."

This phrase "Dark but Comely" reminds us of the words of the maiden girl in the Hebrew book Song of Solomon in Chapter One, verses 5 & 6:

"I am black, but comely, O ye daughters of Jerusalem, as the tents of Kedar, as the curtains of Solomon.

Look not upon me, because I am swarthy, because the sun hath looked upon me: my mother's children were angry with me; they made me the keeper of the vineyards; but mine own vineyard have I not kept."

The Shulammite girl of The Song of Solomon likened her swarthy appearance to "the tents of Kedar", these likely being made of black goat's hair, as are the tents of many modern-day Bedouin. The word *Swarthy* in verse six comes from the Hebrew word Shacharuwth "*shakh-ar-ooth*" which means Swarthy - Black. The word *Comely* according to Strong's Concordance comes from the Hebrew word Naveh "*Naw-veh*" which means Suitable, or Beautiful. Some translators render the word Lovely.

The maiden girl says: "I am black." Some translations render it "I am dark." We notice in chapter 24 of the Pikei DeRabbi Eliezer it says of Shem and his sons that they were "dark but comely" and of

Ham and his sons "dark like the raven." Strong's Concordance says the word for *dark* or *black* in verse five comes from the Hebrew word Shachor, "*shaw-khore*" or Shachowr "*shaw-khore*" prep. "dusky", but also (absol.) "Jetty" - black."

(See Notes)

Adam and Eve, who were once perfect in the Garden of Eden, but the serpent caused them to sin, leading to the first prophecy of a Coming Seed

Israelites making bricks in Egypt. Painting found inside the tomb of Rekhmire, a vizier to King Tuthmosis III in 15th Century BCE

Photos | 57

The Israelite Midwives, who saved the male babies in the Line of Judah.

Mesopotamia region, including Babel & Shinar

Map of West Africa in 1819

Village of Yahoodee, 1819

Kandake Amanitore, Queen of Kush in 1st Century CE. May have been the "Candace" queen whom the Ethiopian eunuch official was serving under during his trip to Jerusalem and subsequent baptism.

60 | The Line of Shem and the Seed of Judah

King Ahasuerus of Persia (Xerxes I) During his reign an edict was passed to exterminate all Jews in his realm, including the Jews in Ethiopia. His wife Queen Esther, and her cousin Mordecai, helped prevent the planned genocide.

CHAPTER 5

Biblical and Historical References to African & Arab Hebrews

In 1898 archaeologists found in a temple at Thebes a black granite pillar that boasts of the achievements of Egyptian King Merneptah of the 19th Dynasty, believed to have reigned in the late 13th Century BCE. Inscribed on the stela are these words: "Israel is laid waste, his seed is no more." This is the only known reference to the nation of Israel in ancient Egyptian texts thus far, and the earliest reference to Israel outside the Bible. The stela was made during the period of the Judges, the time period right after the Israelites under Joshua entered the land of Canaan and divided the land into twelve territories.

The name "Israel" refers not only to the name that Yehovah gave to Jacob, but also to all of his descendants from his twelve sons. During the time of King Saul the terms "Israel" and "Hebrews" were equivalent. The designation "Hebrew" was already familiar to the Egyptians during the time of Abraham in the 18th century BCE. (Ge 39:13, 14, 17; 41:12; Ex 1:16; 1Sa 4:6, 9; Ge 40:15; Ex 1:19; 2:7; Ge 43:32; Ex 1:15; 2:11-13; 1Sa 13:3-7).

This would seem to indicate that Abraham, Isaac, and Jacob had become quite well known in the region. When Joseph spoke of "the land of the Hebrews" (Ge 40:15) to Pharaoh's servants, he no doubt referred to the region around Hebron that his father and forefathers had settled in. The Philistines still spoke of the Israelites as "Hebrews" some six centuries later.

The term "Hebrew" seems to comes from the name Eber ('E'ver), the great-grandson of Shem and an ancestor of Abraham. (Ge 11:10-26) Nothing is known about Eber aside from his family relationship as a link in the chain of descent from Shem to Abraham. It is striking that Eber is specifically singled out at Genesis 10:21, as Shem is being spoken of as "the forefather of all the sons of Eber", as there is no recorded account or personal story about Eber. The use of his name as a patronymic links the Israelites with Shem and Noah (Genesis 10:1-32). The fact that Eber is singled out in the genealogical list of Shem is divine indication that the line of descent of the promised Seed mentioned in Yehovah's prophecy at Genesis 3:15, is a specific link between Shem and Abraham.

The name E'ber comes from a root meaning "pass over (cross)"; or, "other side, opposite side." Eber is used at Numbers 24:24 as either referring to the Hebrew race or to a region. The Greek Septuagint, the Syriac Peshitta, and the Latin Vulgate here render "Eber" as "the Hebrews." This scriptural text applies Eber's name to a certain people or region centuries after his death. The text may be referring to the land or people on the other side of the Euphrates.

Yehovah's prophetic utterance was fulfilled in Abraham:

"Your name will no longer be A'bram; your name will become Abraham, for I will make you a father of many nations."

Abraham's son Isaac was by means of his wife Sarah. After Sarah died, Abraham again took a wife, Keturah, and thereafter fathered six additional sons: Zimran, Jokshan, Medan, Midian, Ishbak, and Shuah. And Ishmael was the first son of Abraham by his concubine the Egyptian Hagar. Ishmael was circumcised at the age of 13, along with his father and his father's servants. (Genesis 17:23-27). Isaac later found a wife, Rebekah, and gave birth to Jacob.

It is quite likely that intermarriage between Ishmaelites and the descendants of Abraham through Keturah took place. Since Ishmael and Midian were half-brothers, any intermarriage of their respective descendants resulted in an amalgamation of their genetic blood, traits, and occupations. This might also help explain an interchangeable usage of the terms "Ishmaelites" and "Midianites," as in the case of the caravan that sold Joseph into Egyptian slavery. The Ishmaelites were therefore one fourth Semitic and three fourths Hamitic. Ishmael and Midian may have been much alike in their way of life. Some of the Kenites were also known as Midianites. Zipporah the Midianite, who was the daughter of priest Reuel of the land of Midian, is referred to as a "Cushite", the wife of Moses. Some descendants of Cush, therefore, settled in Arabia.

Ishmael married an Egyptian by whom he had 12 sons: Nebaioth, Kedar, Adbeel, Mibsam, Mishma, Dumah, Massa, Hadad, Tema, Jetur, Naphish, Kedemah. the chieftains of the various Ishmaelite clans. Ishmael also had one known daughter, Mahalath or Basemath, the third wife of Esau.

One of the 12 sons of Ishmael was Kedar (from a root meaning: "be dark"). In the Song of Solomon, the Shulamite girl likened her swarthy appearance to "the tents of Kedar." Goat's hair was used to make "the tent upon the tabernacle." (Exodus 26:7) The tents of Kedar apparently were made of black goat's hair, as is true today from the Bedouin tribe in Palestine.

A particular Hebrew Arab tribe descended from Kedar:

According to tradition, Adnan is the father of a group of the Ishmaelite Arabs who inhabited West and Northern Arabia. Tradition and Muslim scholars state that Adnan is a descendant of Kedar (Qedar) the son of Ishmael, the son of Abraham. From Adnan, the Umayyad Dynasty and the Abbasid Dynasty descended from Abd Manaf. The Umayyad Dynasty were the Moors over Spain.

In 711 the Islamic Arabs and Moors of Berber descent in northern Africa crossed the Strait of Gibraltar onto the Iberian Peninsula, and in a series of raids they conquered Visigothic Christian Hispania. In 756, Abd al-Rahman I, a prince of the deposed Umayyad royal family, refused to recognize the authority of the Abbasid Caliphate and became an independent emir of Córdoba. From the ninth to the tenth century, under the Caliphate of Córdoba, the region was one of the most prosperous and advanced in Europe. It was at this time that the Moorish caliphate reached its zenith and Córdoba, in southern Spain, became a thriving metropolis. The university was a celebrated center of learning, and the city contained a public library containing 400,000 volumes. Twenty-seven free schools were provided to teach poor children. There was a high standard of literacy.

The huge influx of wealth was also reflected in the general appearance of the city. The streets were paved and lighted. Gardens, waterfalls, and ornamental lakes adorned the city, while an aqueduct brought fresh water in abundance to supply the fountains and public baths.

However, in the eleventh century, the Umayyad dynasty came to an end, and there began a series of assassinations, uprisings, and feuds. Over the following centuries Moorish Spain was gradually absorbed by the feudal kingdoms of Spanish Christendom from the north. The Nasrid dynasty was the last Muslim dynasty in Moorish Iberian Spain. Twenty-three emirs ruled Granada from the founding of the dynasty in 1230 by Muhammad I until 2 January 1492, when

Muhammad XII surrendered all lands to King Ferdinand of Aragon and Queen Isabella of Castile.

On March 31, 1492, Ferdinand and Isabella signed an edict, the Alhambra Decree, expelling Jews from Spain. This will be fully discussed in Chapter 12.

When told that Sarah would have a son from whom "kings of peoples" would come, Abraham cried out to the true God in behalf of his firstborn, saying:

> "O that Ish′ma·el might live before you!" To this God said: "Your wife Sarah will definitely bear you a son, and you must name him Isaac. And I will establish my covenant with him for an everlasting covenant to his offspring after him. But as regards Ish′ma·el, I have heard you. Look! I will bless him and will make him fruitful and will multiply him very, very much. He will produce 12 chieftains, and I will make him become a great nation." (Genesis 17:16, 18-20)

Ishmael was present with Isaac at their father Abraham's burial.

CHAPTER 6
King Solomon's Mines

According to the Book of Kings, King Solomon of Judah built a fleet of ships in the Gulf of `Aqaba on the Red Sea at Ezion-geber. King Hiram of Tyre then supplied experienced seamen to navigate them along with Solomon's servants. In addition to these ships that plied the waters off the east coast of Africa, Solomon and Hiram had other ships sailing as far as Tarshish, at the western end of the Mediterranean.

At this location on the gulf Aqaba, Phoenician King Hiram of Tyre, cooperated with Solomon in this enterprise (1 Kings 9:26-28; 10:11). The excavators at Tell el-Kheleifeh found the remains of a massive city gate and a storage depot. This storage depot would have been used to house such items as gold, precious stones, wood and other materials, until they were transported by caravans to their points of destination. The placing of such a storage depot on the gulf at the Red Sea was ingenious, since important sea and land trade routes intersected in that area.

Ham's son Canaan had a firstborn son named Sidon. Sidon's descendants eventually became known as Sidonians. So the Sidonians were actually Canaanites. Sometime prior to the 15th Century BCE the Sidonians established a colony on the Mediterranean coast and named the seaport town Sidon, today the largest city in Lebanon.

Another Sidonian colony was later formed about 22 miles away (35 km) and called Tyre. Both seaports Sidon and Tyre became trading centers where traveling caravans and merchant ships came to engage in trading. The Sidonians became well known for their skills as shipbuilders, metalworkers, artisans, and craftsmen in glassware, weaving, and engraving. The Greeks who sailed into their seaports began calling the Sidonians by the name "Phoenicians."

So where actually was the exact location of Tarshish?

The "fleet of ships of Tarshish" that Solomon had on the sea "along with King Hiram's fleet of ships," were stated in the scriptures to have made voyages once every three years for the importation of gold, silver, ivory, apes, and peacocks. Tarshish was said to have exported vast quantities of important metals to Phoenicia and Israel. Hebrew biblical passages point to Tarshish as a source of King Solomon's great wealth in metals, which included also tin and iron.

The Phoenicians were a people from the eastern Mediterranean who were sea-faring traders from the cities of Tyre and Sidon. They established many trading colonies around the Mediterranean, including the colony of Carthage, which was founded in the year 814 BC, on the North African coast in what is now Tunisia.

Carthage later grew to become the most powerful Phoenician city in the Mediterranean. Carthage controlled Southern Iberia (Spain, Portugal), and the islands of Sicily, Sardinia, Corsica, and Malta, and several colonies.

At Romans 15:24: Paul said:

"I plan to do so when I go to *Spain*. I hope to see you while passing through and to have you assist me on my journey there, after I have enjoyed your company for a while."

At the time that Paul mentioned of his intent to journey there, Spain had become a province of Rome. Present-day Merida, Spain was known as the Emerita Augusta, a colony founded for the retired soldiers who fought for the Emperor Augustus in 25 BCE. It later became the capital of the Roman Republic province of *Hispania Ulterior*. An early province governor was the future Roman Emperor Marcus Salvius Otho, who ruled Rome for a mere three months, January-April 69 CE. The year 69 CE is known as *the Year of Four Emperors*. Emperor Nero committed suicide in 68 CE, a mercy killing by his personal servant. Upon Nero's death, Servius Sulpicius Galba became the next Emperor. He lasted 7 months until he was assassinated and replaced by Otho.

Otho barely lasted 3 months. He was replaced by Aulus Vitellius, who ruled 8 months before he was replaced by Army Commander Titus Flavius Vespasian, who was in the middle of suppressing the Jewish revolt in Judea beginning in 66 CE. When Vespasian was declared Emperor, he left his son General Titus Vespasianus in charge of ending the Jewish rebellion, which he did in 70 CE. An ancient pedestal of a golden statue to Emperor Titus (he became emperor after his father's death) was found in Merida and now in the Museum of Madrid. Finally, Emperor Vespasian granted *ius Latii* (Roman citizenship) to the whole Roman province of Hispania.

The Greek Septuagint scrolls render Tarshish as *Carthage*. Most scholars associate Tarshish with the southern region of Spain, once ruled by Carthage, based on ancient references to a place or region called *Tartessus* by Greek and Roman writers. Greek geographer Strabo of the first century BCE placed a city called Tartessos in the region around the Guadalquivir River in Andalusia. Pausanias, writing in the 2nd century CE, identified the river and gave details of the location of the city:

"They say that Tartessus is a river in the land of the Iberians, running down into the sea by two mouths and that between these two mouths lies a city of the same name. The river, which is the largest in Iberia and tidal, those of a later day called Baetis."

The Baetis river is today the Guadalquivir. How do we know? In Latin, *Baetica* is an adjectival form of Baetis, the name the Romans called the Guadalquivir River. Hispania Baetica was one of three Roman provinces in Spain until the Visigoths by the 5th Century CE.

Further, Cádiz, a city and port in southwestern Spain, was founded by the Phoenicians around 1100 century BCE and is one of the oldest continuously inhabited cities in Southern Europe. In Latin, the city was known as *Gādēs*. In Arabic, the name became *Qādis*, from which the Spanish *Cádiz* derives. The expeditions of Himilco around Spain and France and of Hanno around Western Africa began there. The Phoenicians at Cadiz traded with Tartessos.

So this solves the mystery of the location of Tarshish/Tartessos. It was in ancient Carthage territory, which later became southern Spain.

All together, these extensive operations from East Africa, India, Orphir, Phoenician colonies, and Tarshish brought in a great deal of wealth—ivory, precious stones, apes, valuable woods, peacocks, silver, and gold. The apes imported by King Solomon may have been a species of long-tailed monkeys referred to by ancient writers as being from Ethiopia. (1Ki 10:22; 2Ch 9:21)

Ebony wood is mentioned only once in the Bible, at Ezekiel 27:15, where it is presented as an item of commerce. The ebony and ivory there mentioned were brought out of India or Sri Lanka, perhaps across the Arabian Sea and up the Red Sea and then overland, or else from Nubia. It was highly sought by the ancient Egyptians. Solomon made a great ivory throne and overlaid it with refined gold. The city of Tyre, in her great sea commerce, inlaid the prows of her ships with ivory. The African bush elephant, also known as the African savanna elephant, is one of two extant African elephant species. It is the largest living terrestrial animal. The other is the North African elephant, which existed in North Africa. These were the famous war elephants used by Carthage in the Punic Wars. Ivory also came from India to Solomon's courts.

Algum trees were included by Solomon in his request to Hiram of Tyre for timbers for the construction of the temple. Hiram brought them from Ophir, as it was a trading center dealing with India, Egypt, and other places in Africa. Commercial trade existed between India and Africa even before Solomon's time.

Large amounts of gold poured into Solomon's treasury from the king of Tyre (120 talents) and the queen of Sheba (120 talents), from annual tributes and taxes, and by means of his own merchant fleet. The scriptures say: "The weight of the gold that came to Solomon in one year amounted up to six hundred and sixty-six talents of gold."

Ophir was a place renowned as a source of much gold of the finest quality. "Pure gold" were spoken of in parallel with the "gold of Ophir." David donated 3,000 talents of gold from Ophir for construction of the temple. (1Ch 29:1,2,4) Later, the trading fleet of Solomon regularly brought back from Ophir 420 talents of gold. (1Kings 9:26-28)

But where else might King Solomon have procured his gold?

The Ghana Empire produced so much gold that the tenth-century Persian geographer Ibn al-Faqih claimed that gold grew "in the sand, as carrots do, and is picked at sunrise." The Muslim historian al-Bakri wrote in the eleventh century how the dogs in Ghana wore "golden collars" and horses had golden saddles.

Nahum Slouschz mentions in his *Travels in North Africa*: "The traditions of the Jewish trader in the Sahara *stretch back to biblical times*. He goes on to state: "And it is not at all surprising to encounter in every part of the desert traces – and even survivals – of a primitive Judaism which at one time played an important role in the whole region of the Sahara *from Senegal to the very borders of Somaliland.*"

This stretch of land from West Africa to East Africa below the Sahara is known as the Sudan. (See Notes)

The **Wangara** (also known as Wakore, Wankori, Dyula) were part of the Soninke people. They were merchants who operated across the Sudan-Sahel.

The Wangara are described as Malians who specialized in long-distance commerce, and were the first link in the chain that reached from the producers of gold in West Africa to the Mediterranean. The Wangara kept the location of the gold mines a secret to protect their monopoly.

The gold trade was a foundation of Carthage. They used Berber nomads to establish a trade route across the Sahara to the goldfields of Bambuk in the Senegal River valley. (See Notes)

Hanno the Navigator was a Carthage explorer of the 5th century BCE. Carthage dispatched Hanno at the head of a fleet of 60 ships to explore the northwestern coast of Africa. He sailed from Cadiz, Carthage, founded or repopulated seven colonies along the African coast of what is now Morocco, and reached Senegal. Some researchers say he continued past Senegal and reached Cameroon. So Hanno achieved a circumnavigation of Africa. Hanno's account, the *Periplus*, remains extant in Greek-language manuscripts. The original version has been lost. The *Periplus* survives as one of the few extant accounts of ancient exploration written by the explorer himself:

> "THE VOYAGE OF HANNO,
> KING OF THE CARTHAGINIANS
> "To the Libyan regions of the earth beyond the
> Pillars of Hercules, which he dedicated also
> in the Temple of Baal, affixing this

"It pleased the Carthaginians that Hanno should voyage outside the Pillars of Hercules, and found cities of the Libyphœnicians. And he set forth with sixty ships of fifty oars, and a multitude of men and women, to the number of thirty thousand, and with wheat and other provisions.

"Sailing thence we came to the **Lixus**, a great river flowing from Libya. By it a wandering people, the Lixitas, were pasturing their flocks; with whom we remained some time, becoming friends.

"Taking interpreters from them, we sailed twelve days toward the south along a desert, turning thence toward the east one day's sail. There, within the recess of a bay we found a small island, having a circuit of fifteen stadia; which we settled, and called it **Cerne**. From our journey we judged it to be situated opposite Carthage ; for the voyage from Carthage to the Pillars and thence to Cerne was the same.

"Sailing thence, we came to **another river, very great** and broad, which was full of crocodiles and hippopotami. And then we turned about and went back to Cerne.

> "But on the last day we came to **great wooded mountains**. The wood of the trees was fragrant, and of various kinds.
>
> "Sailing around these mountains for two days, we came to an **immense opening of the sea,** from either side of which there was level ground inland; from which at night we saw fire leaping up on every side at intervals, now greater, now less."

Hanno makes mention of a very great river full of crocodiles and hippopotami. This river is the Senegal. Hanno then mentions of great wooded mountains. This is Cape Verde. Finally, he records an immense opening of the sea. Hanno is describing the mouth of the Gambia river. (See Notes)

King Necho of Egypt also commissioned the Phoenicians. King Necho was a king of the 26th Dynasty in the 7th century BCE. At some point between 610 and before 594 BC, the length of his reign, Necho commissioned an expedition of Phoenicians, who in three years completed a circumnavigation around Africa from the Red Sea to Gibraltar and back to the mouth of the Nile.

Herodotus wrote of this feat:

> "For my part I am astonished that men should ever have divided Libya, Asia, and Europe as they have, for they are exceedingly unequal. Europe extends the entire length of the other two, and for breadth will not even (as I think) bear to be compared to them. As for Libya, we know it to be washed on all sides by the sea, except where it is attached to Asia. This discovery was first made by Necos, the Egyptian king, who on desisting from the canal which he had begun between the Nile and the Arabian gulf, sent to sea a number of ships manned by Phoenicians, with orders to make for

the Pillars of Hercules, and return to Egypt through them, and by the Mediterranean. The Phoenicians took their departure from Egypt by way of the Erythraean sea, and so sailed into the Southern ocean. When autumn came, they went ashore, wherever they might happen to be, and having sown a tract of land with corn, waited until the grain was fit to cut. Having reaped it, they again set sail; and thus it came to pass that two whole years went by, and it was not till the third year that they doubled the Pillars of Hercules, and made good their voyage home. On their return, they declared - I for my part do not believe them, but perhaps others may - that in sailing round Libya they had the sun upon their right hand. In this way was the extent of Libya first discovered."

George Rawlinson said: "The Phœnicians for some centuries confined their navigation within the limits of the Mediterranean, the Propontis, and the Euxine, land-locked seas, which are tideless and far less rough than the open ocean. *But before the time of Solomon they had passed the Pillars of Hercules and affronted the dangers of the Atlantic.*" (See Notes)

If Necho and Hanno were able to circumnavigate around the continent of Africa, are we to rule out that King Solomon could not have done so, the wisest man on earth, equipped with his fleet of the finest of Phoenician ships? But, the question still begs to be answered: Where else might King Solomon have obtained gold? Did part of his gold reserves come from West Africa? Please consider the following accounts, as they shall fit together in answer of our question.

The *Periplus of Pseudo-Scylax* was written sometime from the mid-4th Century BCE by a Greek geographer named Pseudo-Scylax.

His description is of the sea route starting in Iberia and ending in West Africa. What is important about this particular periplus is that Scylax relates there was an established trade in his day around 350 BCE between Phoenicia and an island called Cerne, off the West African coast. Scylax says:

> "The merchants who are Phoenicians, when they have arrived at Cerne, anchor their vessels there, and after having pitched their tents upon the shore, proceed to unload their cargo, and to convey it in smaller boats to the mainland. *The dealers with whom they trade are Ethiopians*; and these dealers sell to the Phoenicians skins of deer, lions, panthers, and domestic animals—elephants' skins also, and their teeth. The Ethiopians wear embroidered garments, and use ivory cups as drinking vessels; their women adorn themselves with ivory bracelets; and their horses also are adorned with ivory… These Ethiopians are eaters of flesh and drinkers of milk; they make also much wine from the vine; and the Phoenicians, too, supply some wine to them. *They have a considerable city, to which the Phoenicians sail up.*"

Notice that Scylax mentions that Ethiopians traveled to meet the Phoenician merchants near the island of Cerne on the coast of West Africa to engage in trade. Scylax also noted that "the Phoenicians sail up" to the Ethiopians' city. Ethiopia was known for her gold. We can deduce from this account that Ethiopians may have easily acquired their gold from West Africa as well.

Herodotus mentions the gold trade between Carthage and West Africa:

"Another story is told by the Carthaginians. There is a place in Libya, they say, where men live beyond the Pillars of Heracles; they come here and unload their cargo; then, having laid it in order along the beach, they go aboard their ships and light a smoking fire. The people of the country see the smoke, and, coming to the sea, **they lay down gold to pay for the cargo**, and withdraw from the wares. Then the Carthaginians disembark and examine the gold; if it seems to them a fair price for their cargo, they take it and go away; but if not, they go back aboard and wait, **and the people come back and add more gold until the sailors are satisfied**. In this transaction, it is said, neither party defrauds the other: the Carthaginians do not touch the gold until it equals the value of their cargo, nor do the people touch the cargo until the sailors have taken the gold."

Another tribe encountered on the trade routes were the Garamantes. The Garamantes were a Berber tribe who lived almost directly south of what would become Carthage and would control the trade going into and coming out of the Sahara from West Africa. The Garamantes determined the trade across the desert. Herodotus mentions them:

"Ten days' journey from Augila there is again a **salt-hill** and a spring; palms of the fruitful kind grow here abundantly, as they do also at the other salt-hills. This region is inhabited by a nation called the Garamantians, a very powerful people, who cover the salt with mould, and then sow their crops… "The Garamantians have four-horse chariots, in which they chase the Troglodyte Ethiopians, who of all the nations whereof any account has reached our ears are by far the swiftest of foot."

This account mentions salt. We cannot forget the salt trade in West Africa. Salt and Gold went hand in hand. Salt from the Sahara was one of the major trading goods of ancient West Africa. The most common exchange was gold for salt and vice versa. Salt was in great demand, as it was a preservative for meat and other foods. Without question the Garamantes engaged in such commercial business on the trade routes. (See Notes)

Thus, we can confidently conclude, as we fit together all these different accounts, that one of the gold mines that King Solomon utilized for his gold reserves were very possibly sourced from the gold supply-link of West Africa, whether it was brought to Tarshish or Cadiz and obtained there, or transported by caravan through the Sudan and ending at the depot at Ezion-Geber, Solomon's shipping base on the Red Sea.

We will again revisit yet another discussion involving expeditions by sea later on in Chapter 13, as the death-dealing journey of Columbus and the slave ships, which further scattered the remaining descendants of Israel, will be examined. It will reveal proof as to the *real reason* why Columbus took his 3rd voyage. For decades this proof is something historians have either accidentally overlooked, or deliberately fail to acknowledge.

CHAPTER 7

Shem & Ham In the Land of China

Branches of both the line of Shem and of the Line of Ham entered Indo-China during its early history. Descendants of the Jews are still in China and India today. These descendants must be located, so that they too may be told the full and complete understanding of the Most High's prophecy in Eden, about the coming foretold Seed of Judah.

Let us begin first with how the Hebrew Jews came into China.

In the province of Henan, in the city called Kaifeng, is an old Jewish synagogue dating back to 1163. In the courtyard of the synagogue were four steles (now in the Kaifeng Museum and in the Biblotheque Mission in Shanghai) written in Chinese characters by the Jewish community at that time, which detailed the history of their origin. The first stele was created in 1489, and the second in 1512 (written on the backside of the 1489 stele). The third and fourth steles were written in 1663 and 1679. The Jesuits documented this Jewish community when coming upon them in the early 1600's. As to the origin of these Jews who arrived in Kaifeng, part of the 1489 stele reveals this:

> "Now Issuloyeh (Israel) established the religion Awulohan (Abraham) the Patriarch was the 19th generation descended

from Atan (Adam) …he established the religion the origin of which was transmitted to now

Examining it, it was the 146th year of the Tcheou (Zhou) Dynasty

Once transmitted, it reached Moses, the Patriarch of the religion

Examining it, it was the 613th year of the Tcheou (Zhou)…"

The 1512 stele proclaims this:

"After the Creation the Doctrine was transmitted by Adam to Nuwa (Noah); thence unto Awulohan, Issuhako, and Yahochuehwu (Abraham Issac and Jacob), and afterwards through the twelve patriarchs to Miehshe, Aholien, and Yuehshuwo (Moses, Aaron, and Joshua). Aitzula (Ezra) promulgated the Law, and through him the letters of the Yuethe (Yehudi) nation, were made plain."

The 1663 stele adds this detail:

"The religion started in Tienchu (India) and was first transmitted to China during the Chou (Zhou)…Through the Han, T'sang, Sung, Ming, and up till now, it has undergone many vicissitudes."

Combining all of the above-referenced quotes tell us several things. (See Notes)

First, we notice from the 1512 stele that the name adopted for Noah was Nuwa. The Chinese were acquainted with the name Nuwa, for in their Chinese mythology Nuwa was a sovereign who, according to their legend, mended the skies with five-colored stones to stop the flooding waters that were coming upon the earth. Here we find again another legend of the global deluge, which did truly occur in the days of Noah. The colors of the rainbow were an eternal sign from the Most High that He would never destroy the world by water ever again.

Secondly, the 1489 stele states that the Jewish Kaifeng community believed that Awulohan - Abraham - established their worship and way of life, and that he had examined the origin of their worship in the 146th year of the Zhou dynasty, and next Moses examined it in the 613th year of the Zhou. So, when was the Zhou dynasty? And can these years be determined from the Zhou history?

Being that the time period of the Zhou dynasty differs among various lettered scholars, it would be mere speculation to try and determine precisely the corresponding 146th and 613th years of that dynasty. Some say the Zhou ruled from 1050 - 221 BCE. Others say 1100 - 221 BCE. The major consensus say the period of the Zhou was more closer to 1046 - 256 BCE.

Be that it may, one should not ignore or forget the far more important point: What did the Kaifeng Jews *themselves* understand the time period to be? They are the ones who wrote the stele. No one has that definitive answer yet.

However, there is one promising observation from the 1489 stele that goes to the heart of when this group of Jews first entered China: it occurred *during* the Zhou reign. And the fact that mention is made of the "146th year" and the "613th year" seems to imply that at least two waves of Jewish settlement possibly occurred.

Another realization is also concrete clear; whether one accepts any of the proposed time periods of the Zhou - whether 1100-221

BCE, or 1050-221 BCE, or 1046-256 BCE - all of these dates are inclusive of two other contemporaneous ruling powers: The reign of King Solomon, and the rule of the Persian Empire.

The reign of King Solomon, son of David, over the twelve tribes of Israel, ran from 1037-998 BCE; And the period of the Persian empire was 550-330 BCE, when soon they were conquered by Alexander the Great. The Persian kingdom and the Most High's earthly kingdom under the anointed King Solomon – both were ruling during the time of the Zhou dynasty at different stages.

As discussed in Chapter 6, King Solomon held a vast fleet of ships manned by both Judean and Phoenician sailors. Every three years, the ships of Solomon along with the ships of King Hiram of Tyre partnered together and sailed around the then-known world to procure all types of desirable merchandise and valuable trade items.

There is no reason to doubt that Solomon's ships sailed into the ports of China, and India, or that his royal trading merchants would not have sought after the markets of the Indo-China region.

Silk was sought after in biblical times. Ancient China was noted for its use of the Chinese silkworm in its production of silk. Traders came to acquire it. Silken fabric, considered by archaeologists to have been woven over 2,000 years ago, has been found in tombs of a Phoenician cemetery near Sabrata, Libya. The trading route known as the Great Silk Road ran from China to the Mediterranean. More than a thousand years before Vasco de Gama in 1497, ships sailed over the Indian Ocean and the Red Sea between Egypt. Ancient land routes connected Southeast Asia, China, and India to Arabia, East Africa, and Egypt, which was a link to the Palestine region. In Mesopotamia, during the same time period as the Zhou, east Indian traders had their settlement. Ebony, ivory, and cotton, including silk, for use in the technique of Egyptian mummy-wrapping, were supplied to Egypt in the second millennium BCE by Abyssinian and Somali traders who transported them from India. (See Notes)

The northern 10-Tribe Kingdom of Israel in all likelihood also participated in the silk trade and imported it during the reign of bad King Jeroboam II, son of Jehoash and great-grandson of Jehu. This was greatly due to Jeroboam restoring land back to the kingdom which had earlier been lost, including the land of Damascus, who engaged in silk importing. The prophet Amos, who lived during Jeroboam's reign, uttered a warning to Samaria:

> "This is what Yehovah says, Just as a Shephard snatches away two legs or a piece of an ear from the mouth of the lion, that is how the people of Israel will be snatched away, those now sitting in Samaria on splendid beds and on *Damascene* couches."

Rotherham's translation says: "and on the *silken* cushions of a bed", showing that Damascus was noted for its reputation in silk dealings. Now that Jeroboam had made Damascus a part of his kingdom territory, Israel would also now bask in its material prosperity.

Many trade routes previously established under the Roman Empire and prior, continued to function. the Radhanite mechants during the 8th and 9th centuries also traveled into China and India on these previously established trade routes prior to the Silk Route Road, obtaining spices, perfumes, furs, and silk.

Turning to the Persian Empire, it too was a ruling power during parts of the time period of the Zhou dynasty. In the year 520 BCE, King Darius Hystaspis, also called Darius the Great, sent orders to Tattenai, the Persian governor of the region west of the Euphrates, to lift the ban that had been placed on the Jews' work of rebuilding the temple in Jerusalem, which they had begun in 537 BCE by Cyrus' permission. Darius ordered officials to not only refrain from interfering with the temple work but also provide building funds from the royal treasury, as well as animals and other necessary supplies for the sacrificial offerings. Anyone violating the king's order was to be impaled on a stake and his house "turned into a public privy." The work resumed and the Jews completed building the temple in 515 BCE. However, not all of the Hebrew Jews had left Persia and returned to Jerusalem, their homeland. Why? Had not Cyrus freed them from the 70-year yoke under the Babylonians, as foretold by the Most High?

Many of the Jews had become prosperous in Babylon while they were in captivity, and to leave the comforts they had built up and return to Jerusalem to start over became a conflicting decision for some. Returning to Jerusalem meant for some a loss of position and connections in Babylon, which had become their home. For some Jews it may have been the only home they knew, as many were born in Babylon, now under Persian rule. On the other hand, there were elderly Jews with failing health, who may have felt they were too old to endure a hard, long journey. No doubt it would take strong faith to take the journey to Jerusalem, and possibly a dangerous journey if enemies or aggressive tribes might be encountered.

The walls of Jerusalem were still unfinished. There were huge gaps left in them where the gates had been burnt and not repaired. (See Notes) The Temple, though completed, still the inside furnishings and its ornaments were inadequate. Only some 1,500 men and their families were found willing and able to go, perhaps 6,000 in total number went with Ezra.

Some went with Zerubbabel in 537 BCE. Some went also with High Priest Ezra in 468 BCE. And some went with Nehemiah in 455 BCE. But not all of God's people chose to return to their homeland.

Darius Hystaspis before his death extended the borders of Persia into India. That is why the Hebrew scriptures say in the Book of Esther: "Now it came to pass in the days of Ahasuerus, this is Ahasuerus which reigned, from *India* even unto Ethiopia, over a hundred and seven and twenty provinces." Darius Hystaspis then died in 486 BCE, and his son Ahasuerus Xerxes I succeeded him. Xerxes was also known as Xerxes Longimanus, because his right hand was longer than his left.

Evidence shows that Darius Hystaspis and his son Xerxes Longimanus ruled Persia together as a co-regency, until 486 BCE when his son succeeded him.

Ahasuerus Xerxes Longimanus was the Persian king mentioned in the Book of Esther. He deposed his wife, Queen Vashti, and chose the Hebrew Esther to become his new wife and queen. Duped by evil Haman, King Xerxes passed a law authorizing genocide upon the Jews in all of Persia's provinces, including Jews in Ethiopia and India. At the last minute, the genocidal plot was frustrated and Haman was executed.

Over thirteen hundred years later in the 9th Century CE, Hebrew Jews were documented by two Mohammedan merchants living in China named Abu Zayd Hasan ibn Yazid Sirafi and Sulaiman al-Tajir. Their observations are mentioned in the book *Ancient Accounts of India and China*:

> "And yet there is a great number of Jews in China, as may be gathered from our two Authors, and the rather as they are still in several Provinces, but particularly in the Trading Cities."

In the year 878 CE, there was a massacre in Khanfu, China, known today as Guangzhou, in which many Jews were killed, as the two merchants recalled:

> "Besides the Chinese, who were massacred upon this Occasion, there perished one Hundred and Twenty Thousand Mohammedans, Jews, Christians, and Parsees, who were there on Account of Traffic…Our Authors observe that in the general Devastation of China, and particularly when Canfu was taken, a great number of…Jews…were put to the Sword." (See Notes)

In conclusion, it is very likely that while during the Achaemenid Empire, waves of Hebrew Jews migrated into the Indo-China region from Persia, as well as Judean royal agents during the reign of King Solomon in the 11th century BCE.

Now let us explore how and when the Line of Ham entered China and SE Asia.

Ham, the son of Noah, whose name means *the Burnt One*. Strong's Concordance shows the name Ham in Hebrew is also *Cham*, meaning warm, hot. In Egyptian the name is *Khem*, after whose name the land of Egypt was called *Kemet*, "*In connection with the Sun*" or "*the black land*." (See Notes)

When did *Ham* and China first make contact with each other?

East African merchant Zhengjiani and his trade party traveled to China in 1071 and was received by Chinese Emperor Shenzong. The emperor gave Zhengjiani the title "Lord Guardian of Prosperity", revealing the deep bonds of trade and commerce between the two of them. Zhengjiani and his merchant delegates returned again to China in 1081.

The Chinese admiral and navigator Zheng He explored the coast of East Africa in the year 1416 during the Ming Dynasty, and visited Mogadishu, present-day Somalia. Zheng He's sailing charts of forty pages, called the *Mao Kun* Map, cover four areas – Sri Lanka, South India, Maldives, and 400 kilometers of the east coast of Africa. The ancient Chinese also developed, during the Ming Dynasty, a map of the African continent in 1389, which is noted for including the southern tip of the continent around present-day South Africa. These facts show that cartography of Africa existed in ancient China.

In the year 813, according to the Chinese archives of the Tang Dynasty, in the *New Dynastic History of T'ang*, Book CCXXII, under the section *The Ho-ling Kuo Tiao* is found the following entry:

"In the eighth year of the Yuan Ho period, the land of Ho-ling presented four Seng-chih slaves."

This Chinese document contains an important clue. On the East coast of Africa is the country Zanzibar, settled by Bantu-speakers during the first millennium and originally called *Zanj* which means *Country of the Blacks*. Zanj for centuries shipped slaves to many kingdoms bordering the Indian Ocean. Those enslaved and traded to these countries were also referred to as *Zanj* slaves, designating their origin. The supply of slaves coming out of East Africa was part of the East African Slave Trade that flourished for centuries, even longer than the Atlantic Slave Trade. That official entry in the archives of the Tang Dynasty during the year 813 reveals that the four enslaved servants China received were from Zanj. The land of *Ho-ling* who presented China with four servants was the present-day country of Java in Indonesia. The regional trading routes of Zanj, or Zanzibar, stretched not only to China, but even to the Indonesian islands and

Iran (Persia). This also demonstrates that both China and Africa shared mutual interests in the Indian Ocean trade.

Another word used in China to describe a person who was black and dark-skinned or a dark-skinned slave was the Chinese word *Kunlun*, found in their fiction and nonfiction literature.

In the *Chu Fan Chih* (Information about Barbarians) during the year 1226, the following entry show the words Kunlun and Zanj combined together:

> "The Land of **K'un-lun Ts'eng-ch'i** is situated on the shores of the Southwestern Sea behind a screen of large islands… the products of the land consist of elephant tusks and rhinoceros' horns. To the west there is an island peopled with savages whose complexion is like black lacquer and whose tresses resemble wriggling tadpoles. They are captured by using food as a bait, and are sold at great profit to the Arabs as slaves. The Arabs entrust them with their keys, knowing that they will be faithful be-cause they have no kith nor kin."

During the time of the Liu Song Dynasty in the fifth century, the term Kunlun was mentioned in an account about a Kunlun slave named Bai Zhu, who stood at the emperor's side and who took orders from the emperor to beat ministers and officials with a stick. The name Bai was a common surname for non-Chinese people. Another example is found in a famous romance novel in China, written by Pei Xing in 880, called "The Kunlum Slave", when the black slave Mo-le, and his superhuman strength, rushes to save Cui's lover from the harem of a court official. The slave Mo-le leaped over ten walls with both of them on his back to safety. When the official learns of the escape he orders Mo-le to be captured, but Mo-le jumps over the city walls and is never seen again until ten years later selling medicine in the city.

However, were the presence of East Africans living in China only due to slavery? Did the word "Kunlun" apply only to African slaves? From the Chinese archives, the *Lin-yi Kuo Chuan*, ("Topography of the Land of Linyi") contained in Book 197 of the *Chiu T'ang Shu* ("Old Dynastic History of T'ang") in the year 945 said this:

> "The people living to the south of Linyi have woolly hair and black skin, and are commonly known as K'unlun."

In the section titled *Chen-la Kuo Chuan* (Topography of the Land of Chen-la) found in the same book *Chiu Tang Shu*, we find the following:

> "Chen-la is situated to the north-west of Lin-yi. It was formerly a dependency of Fu Nan. Its inhabitants belong to the race of K'un-lun."

The land of Linyi was Vietnam, and Chen-la represented the Khmer Empire, which later became Cambodia and parts of Vietnam, Laos, and Thailand. In volume X of the same work, we read: "**The northern frontier of the land of K'un-lun…The country abounds in ebony, sandalwood, spices, glazed wares, crystal, medicinal herbs, precious stones.**" (See Notes)

In the *Wang Wu Tien Chu Kuo Chuan* (A Record of travels in the Five Indies) by Hui Ch'ao, we read one more reference about Kun-lun: "**To reach India and K'unlun, one must go by way of Gandahara.**" In another section it says: "**Voyages from the Western Sea to the Southern Seas are frequently made for the purpose of procuring precious merchandise from Ceylon and gold from K'unlun, and they even sail as far as Canton to secure silk and other textiles.**"

Another reference is found in the year 684 in the ancient work *Jiu Tang shu* (Former Tang history), containing the phrase the "Kunlun of Guangzhou" (Canton). All of the above-cited texts clearly show that the word Kunlun referred not only to enslaved Africans, but also referred to Chinese communities in China and also to other Asian peoples. Two questions now arise: Why was the word Kunlun – which was synonymous with dark-skinned Africans – also being applied to populations in China, Southeast Asia and Indonesia? Was there evidence that ancient Chinese people had applied that word to themselves?

During the time of the Jin Dynasty, Emperor Fei was deposed in 371, and so Prime Minister Sima Yu replaced him, becoming the 8th emperor and receiving the official name "Emperor Jianwen" in 372. His reign did not last long. By the summer of that same year Emperor Jianwen became ill and soon died, only a few months after he took the throne. His younger concubine wife Li Lingrong out-lived him, who later became Empress dowager in 394 at the age of forty-three. But what is of more interesting note about Empress dowager Li is what the Jin archives recorded about her. According to the History of the Jin, it described Empress Li this way: **"She was tall and her coloring was black. All the people in the palace used to call her Kunlun."** (**See Notes**) Here we find direct evidence that the word "Kunlun" was applied to a Chinese person, even a Chinese Imperial Empress. How did Empress Li originally become a part of the Emperor Jianwen's royal house? Li Lingrong, born in 351, had become a servant girl in his household as a weaver. After the Emperor's concubines were no longer able to conceive, Li Lingrong was selected to become his next concubine and conceive his heir, at the age of ten. She produced two sons and a daughter during their relationship.

So as early as the 4th Century, the word Kunlun applied to dark-skinned Chinese. Empress Li at her death was officially mourned with ceremony pomp and honor by her people, so the word Kunlun carried no negative connotation during that time, since the Chinese Archives made no attempt to hide her physical description of being dark-skinned.

Were early rulers of ancient China the descendants of Ham?

The first Chinese dynasty mentioned in their history is the Xia dynasty (2070-1600 BCE). There are no records that attest to its existence. However, the first *documented* Chinese dynasty is the Shang (1600-1045 BCE), also called the Yin dynasty, which came after the Xia.

After the Shang, came the Zhou dynasty.

The Shang dynasty was contemporary with the time when the Hebrew Israelites were enslaved under the Pharaoh of Egypt. Moses wrote both the Book of Exodus (1513 BCE) and the Book of Job (1473 BCE) during the Shang's reign. One of Job's three companions was Bildad, who was a descendant of Abraham and Keturah's son Shuah. Moses wrote that Job was "the greatest of all the people of the East" at that particular time in history. This means that Job lived after Abraham and Joseph's time.

The legends of the Shang Dynasty associate its origin with a mythical bird. According to the *Annals of the Yin*, in the *Records of the Grand Historian*, the mythical legend of XIE, the founder of the Shang lineage, was miraculously conceived when Jian Di, Emperor Ku's second wife, swallowed an egg dropped by a Bird. Interestingly, the records said the bird was *Xuan Niao*, which means *Black Bird*.

The *Book of Songs* or the *Shi jing* is a collection of songs originating in the Shang and Zhou dynasties, which was part of The Confucian Classics, a canon of important writings reflecting the teachings of Confucius (551-479 BCE).

In the *Book of Songs,* Xie, the founder of the Shang lineage, is called *Xuan wang* 玄王, which means the *Black King*.

The Yellow River is considered the birthplace of ancient Chinese, and, by extension Far Eastern civilization. It was the most prosperous region in early Chinese history. According to *Records of the Grand Historian* scroll 123, Emperor Wu of Han sent men to find the source of the Yellow River. The men came back saying the source of the river was from a mountain. The name they gave to the mountain was *Kunlun*. in Chinese mythology, Kunlun Mountain is considered the ancestral birthplace of the Ancient Chinese nation. As previously discussed in this chapter, the Chinese word Kunlun meant a black, dark-skinned person.

Today, many in China say the Kunlun mountain is the Bayan Har Mountains, which is the source of the Yellow River, in the basin located in the northern part of the range.

So, in review:

The mythical legend of XIE, the founder of the Shang lineage, was conceived when his mother Jian Di swallowed an egg dropped by a Black Bird: *Xuan Niao*.

In the *Book of Songs*, Xie, the founder of the Shang lineage, is called *Xuan wang*, which means the *Black King*.

 The source of the Yellow River, according to the *Records of the Grand Historian, scroll 123*, came from the *Kunlun* Mountain.

Both the Yellow River and Kunlun Mountain in Chinese folklore are the ancestral birthplace of the Ancient Chinese nation and Far East civilization. (See Notes)

Here are other facts to consider:

American historian J.A. Rogers mentioned of a black tribe in Yunnan Province, China near the Tibet border, citing an article in the

New York Times of November 26, 1933 about a tribal people called the Nashi, the Nakhi, or Naxi, meaning *the Black People*:

"The Nakhis, or "Black People,"…Dr. Rock describes as one of the most extraordinary races or tribes surviving in the world today. They number about 200,000, and have kept alive a culture at least 2,000 years old today."

According to the report, their history went back at least 2,000 years at the time the news article was written. This would date the Nashi to the year 68 BCE, the time of the Western Han Dynasty (which came just after the Shang and Zhou).

So why are the Nashi people not dark-skin in appearance today? This is because of assimilation, and subjugation, which these people experienced over thousands of years.

In recent decades, a series of inscribed hieroglyphs and pictures have been found at Neolithic sites in China, including Jiahu, located in Henan Province near the Yellow River. At the Jiahu site, archaeologists identified eleven shell markings which indicate that this tradition of Hieroglyphs has much deeper roots in ancient Chinese culture than previously considered. They demonstrate a history of sign use in the Yellow River valley during the *Shang period*. This collection of pictographic manuscripts in the Yunnan Provincial Museum of China is considered one of the finest examples of the only living pictographic language in the world today.

These Nashi pictographs differ from Chinese characters, and are compared to **Egyptian and Mayan hieroglyphs**.

There are other examples pointing to evidence of an African presence in early Chinese history, one more example being the dark-skin Yi tribe of China, particularly in Guizhou, Yunnan, and Sichuan territory, who practiced a caste slavery system.

The Yi tribe divided themselves into Black Yi and White Yi. The Black Yi were the highest rank of society. They were the slave-owning class, who owned 60 to 70 percent of the arable land. They claimed their blood to be "pure" and forbade intermarriage with the White Yi or to the Ajia (slaves). Also too – a Black Yi without slaves or a poor Black Yi – was still superior in society than any White Yi, even to a wealthy White Yi. The Black Yi ruled by force. On the other hand, the White Yi were under the slave system, yet they could enjoy some economic independence. They had no freedom of migration, so they could not leave their assigned areas without permission from the Black Yi. They also had no right of ownership, but subject to restrictions by their masters. Although a Black Yi would not kill a White Yi, the Black Yi could still transfer his ownership control over a White Yi. Finally, there were the Ajia, the slaves, who could be sold, purchased, and killed without reprisal. Both the White Yi and Ajia slaves did all the farming and cultivation, while the Black Yi did only the administrative and military work. The Yi tribal slave system finally ended in 1949 during the Chinese Revolution. What is the accepted belief and history of the origin of the Chinese?

Chinese mythology held that the Chinese people were descendants of the Yellow Emperor. The most recent research holds that several different races of humans evolved separately and apart from each other at the same time throughout the continents. Chinese school curriculum teach that they evolved from the "Peking Man." However, in January 2005, a breakthrough study was reported by the China News Service – ***DNA testing proved that the first populations of China were from Africa, particularly from the coast of East Africa.*** The testing study was conducted by Chinese DNA specialist Jin Li, professor of both the National Human Genome Center in Shanghai and the Institute of genetics of Fudan University. Professor

Li said the initial purpose and goal of the study was to try and confirm that the Chinese had evolved from the Chinese homo erectus independently of all humans, and the 12,000 DNA samples from 165 different ethnic groups would prove it Instead, the testing revealed something else – that not even one single person of Chinese descent who participated in the test could be considered as a descendant of homo erectus, because their DNA matched *African ethnic groups*. The Y-chromosome haplotypes of males from all parts of East Asia are derived from ancestral haplotypes that only exist in African populations.

The conclusion: China's ancestors were Hamitic, from the family line of Ham, the brother of Shem, and Japheth. For the first time there is now "scientific evidence" that matches the Chinese archival texts of "Black Emperors" in early Chinese history, and, a definitive explanation for the origin of the word *Kunlun*. Is there a legend in China about a worldwide storm that flooded mankind except for a few survivors? Interestingly, the Chinese word for *ship* in Chinese characters literally means *Eight mouths on a vessel*. This matches the original account Moses wrote, that eight persons survived a global deluge on a large vessel: Noah, his wife, their three sons, and their wives.

Other African haplogroups, such as the *Negrito* would continue to migrate – to the Andaman Islands, the Philippines, Papua New Guinea, the aboriginals of Australia, the Pacific Islands, and the Asiatic Siberians who crossed the Bering into the Americas. When commenting on the DNA study, Professor Li stated the test results showed that all humans from different parts of the world are "very close relatives." This is based on proven genetic science – DNA.

96 | The Line of Shem and the Seed of Judah

Black Chinese girl in Canton, 1869. Author: John Thompson, Welcome Collection, London

Black Chinese woman playing lute, 1869. Author: John Thompson, Welcome Collection, London

Royal Mu family of Nashi/Naxi people, Yunnan, China. Ming dynasty (Library of Congress)

Royal Mu family of Nashi/Naxi people, Yunnan, China. Ming dynasty (Library of Congress)

Map of Southeast Asia

CHAPTER 8

The Five Daughters of Manasseh & Sheerah of Ephraim

The Twelve Tribes of Israel had many faithful, God-fearing, and strong, courageous women among them. Such ones as Deborah, Esther, Ruth, Sarah, Rebekah, Rachel, Rahab, Mary, and the list goes on. This was no different among the women of the tribes of Manasseh and Ephraim, *black & comely*, beautiful. The tribes of Manessah and Ephraim were part Hamitic, being that their ancestress was Asenath, the Egyptian wife of Joseph. Let us highlight two accounts in the Hebrew scriptures about some of these women.

A descendant of Manasseh, Zelophehad had five daughters, Mah′lah, Noah, Hog′lah, Mil′cah, and Tir′zah. During the 40-year wandering in the wilderness, Zelophehad died, due to "his own sin." He had no sons but was survived by his five daughters, all of whom survived to enter the Promised Land. (Numbers 27:1; 1Ch 7:15)

At this time under the Law, a father had to give to the firstborn a double portion of everything that he owned. Land was kept in the possession of the same family from generation to generation, and sons would inherit the land. But Zelophehad had no sons. And the law did not stipulate that daughters could inherit land. When Zelophehad's daughters requested their father's share of the land, a question arose whether they should receive an inheritance. Moses brought their case before Yehovah:

> "Then the daughters of Ze·lo′phe·had, the son of He′pher, the son of Gil′e·ad, the son of Ma′chir, the son of Ma·nas′seh, of the families of Ma·nas′seh the son of Joseph, approached. The names of his daughters were Mah′lah, Noah, Hog′lah, Mil′cah, and Tir′zah. They stood before Moses, El·e·a′zar the priest, the chieftains, and all the assembly at the entrance of the tent of meeting and said: "Our father died in the wilderness, but he was not among the group who banded together against Jehovah, the supporters of Kor′ah, but he died for his own sin and he did not have any sons. Why should the name of our father be lost from his family because he had no son? Give us a possession among our father's brothers." So Moses presented their case before Jehovah.

> "Jehovah then said this to Moses: "The daughters of Ze·lo′phe·had are correct. You should by all means give them the possession as an inheritance among their father's brothers and transfer their father's inheritance to them. And tell the Israelites, 'If a man dies without having a son, you must then cause his inheritance to pass to his daughter. And if he has no daughter, you will give his inheritance to his brothers."

The Most High's decision was that daughters should receive the family inheritance when there were no sons in the family. The decision also stipulated that the daughters had to marry men of their father's tribe so that the inheritance would remain within the tribe of Manessah. Yehovah's decision served as a statute for handling future cases.

Another faithful servant of the Most High was Sheerah of the tribe of Ephraim. The tribe of Ephraim were also part Hamitic, descending from Asenath.

Sheerah is mentioned as building three cities. Although this may have been done by some of her descendants. Nonetheless, how did the scriptures credit her with this accomplishment, and which cities were they?

One city that Sheerah was credited to have built was Uz'zen-she'erah (possibly, Ear of Sheerah or Listen to Sheerah). How she 'built' the city is not stated in the Hebrew scrolls, yet Sheerah must have contributed in some major way to Uz'zen-she'rah's progress and development (1Chronicles 7:22-24). Uzzen-sheerah's location is not definitely known. However, it is believed to be identified with Beit Sira, **a Palestinian village in the central West Bank**, about 14.9 kilometers (9.3 mi) west of Ramallah, and 4 kilometers (2 mi) west of the two other cities Sheerah is said to have built, which are Upper and Lower Beth-horon. The hilltop towns formed part of the southern boundary of the tribe of Ephraim. Today the sites are occupied by two modern villages, the upper: Beit 'Ur el Fauqa (Bet Horon Elyon) and the lower: Beit 'Ur et Tahta (Bet Horon Tahton). Beth-horon, perhaps just one of the towns, was later given to the Levites of the sons of Kohath.

These two towns frequently saw warfare in the days of the Twelve Tribes.

During King Saul's reign, "the road of Beth-horon" was used by the Philistines making raids from Michmash. Later, King Solomon fortified both towns, strengthening them with walls, doors, and bar, to block invading forces from Egypt or Philistia. The most celebrated account, though, is the time when Joshua defeated five Amorite kings, "pursuing them by way of the ascent of Beth-horon." Here Yehovah caused a seemingly miraculous event:

> "And the Holy One threw them into a panic before Israel and slew them with a great slaughter at Gibeon, and chased them along the way that goeth up to Bethhoron, and smote them to Azekah, and unto Makkedah.
>
> "And it came to pass, as they fled from before Israel, and were in the going down to Bethhoron, that the LORD cast down great stones from heaven upon them unto Azekah, and they died: they were more which died with hailstones than they whom the children of Israel slew with the sword.
>
> "Then spake Joshua to the LORD in the day when the LORD delivered up the Amorites before the children of Israel, and he said in the sight of Israel,
>
> "Sun, stand thou still upon Gibeon; and thou, Moon, in the valley of Ajalon.
>
> "And the sun stood still, and the moon stayed, until the people had avenged themselves upon their enemies. Is not this written in the book of Jasher? So the sun stood still in the midst of heaven, and hasted not to go down about a whole day." (Joshua 10:10-13)

The victory was Yehovah's! We can credit Sheerah with the privilege of having this stunning defeat of the Most High's enemies in the very town she helped build, which today still exists in Palestinian territory.

This is a sobering reminder of what the Palestinian people today have endured. Many wonder when will there be peace in that part of the earth.

The history of their current situation is called to mind.

During World War I, the United Kingdom agreed to recognize an Arab State after the war, in exchange for the Sharif of Mecca mobilizing an Arab revolt against the Ottoman Empire. The McMahon-Hussein letters show this. The Arabs' purpose was to create an Arab State stretching from Syria to Yemen. The British promised to recognize it. But when the Arabs learned of the Balfour Declaration and of the 1916 Sykes-Picot Agreement to split and occupy Palestinian territory between Britain and France, the Arabs felt betrayed. Following the end of World War I in 1918, the Ottoman Empire conceded the territories of Palestine and Transjordan. The League of Nations setup a mandate for Palestine, requiring Britain to administrate the territories and to put into effect the Balfour Declaration, calling for a national home for the "Jewish people." A population census was conducted in 1922, in which 83, 794 Jews had already been living in Palestine for decades. There were 590, 890 Muslims living in Palestine in 1922, according to the census. **Some of those Muslims were Jews whose ancestors had converted to Islam hundreds of years ago**. Another census was conducted in 1931, showing 174, 610 Jews residing in Palestine, and 759, 717 Muslims (Again, some Muslims were Jews originally but whose ancestors had converted to Islam). One more census was carried out at the end of the Ottoman Empire in 1945. The figures on that census showed 1,061, 270 Muslims, and 553, 600 Jews in the following regions: Galilee District, Nazareth, Haifa, Samaria District, Jenin, Hebron, Jerusalem, Ramallah, Jaffa, Ramle, Gaza, Beersheba.

The United Nations Special Committee on Palestine was created in May 1947 in response to Great Britain's request that the General Assembly make recommendations under article 10 of the Charter, concerning the future government of Palestine. The committee's report in September 1947 supported the termination of the British Mandate in Palestine and a proposal for a Plan of Partition into two independent states.

On November 29, 1947, the United Nations (which replaced the League of Nations) voted to adopt the Partition Plan for Palestine. The Jewish leadership accepted the plan, whereas the Arab leaders did not. On May 14, 1948, the day before the expiration of the British Mandate, the Arab League again refused to accept the UN Partition Plan, and proclaiming the Arabs' right of self-determination. The British terminated the Mandate at midnight of May 14th. Earlier that same day, the Jewish leadership declared the establishment of the State of Israel. The very next day the Arab-Israeli war began. During the war, around 700,000 Palestinian Arabs and 10,000 Jews were forced to evacuate and were displaced. In the three years following the war, millions of European Jews immigrated to Israel. International recognition of the State of Israel was granted by the United States and Russia almost immediately. Recognition by Great Britain came in 1950.

In contrast, on September 22, 1948, the Arab League proclaimed the All-Palestine Government for the Palestine territory. The United States, Great Britain, and Russia did not recognize this new government, although it was recognized by Egypt, Syria, Lebanon, Iraq, Saudi Arabia, and Yemen. Due to lack of international recognition, the new government was dissolved in 1959. Many years and peace treaties later, including the 1994 Oslo agreement with the Palestine Liberation Organization, and agreements with other parties, such as the Palestinian National Authority, or State of Palestine

– civil wars and killings of innocent civilian lives continued. In the 2006 elections, the political Fatah party lost their majority to the Hamas party. In October 2023, began what has been described as the "darkest chapter in Palestine's history," as fighting broke out again, resulting in the loss of over 15,000 Palestinian lives so far, and a grim humanitarian crisis unfolding as never before.

This sadly illustrates why no one can put their trust in man-made governments and political leaders. None of them can bring about true lasting peace. Only the Most High's Kingdom can bring about true peace on earth, and eliminate forever fighting political factions, genocidal hatreds, and all forms of worldwide terrorist actions.

So again – when will there be true peace in that part of the earth? Honest-hearted descendants of Sheerah are longing for it, more now than ever before. There have been many battles on the roads of Beth-horon. Very soon, there will be a decisive battle for peace on this earth. It will be fought in the "Mountain of Megiddo." We will discuss this in Chapter 15.

(See Notes)

CHAPTER 9

The Relief of Lachish

Housed at the British Museum in London are the Siege of Lachish Reliefs, the sculptured slabs that describe in picture detail the violent battle which took place in 732 BCE between the Judean city of Lachish and the army of Assyria under King Sennacherib.

These wall reliefs were discovered between 1845-1847 by archaeologist Austen Henry Layard in Nineveh, Northern Iraq, and later excavated by Layard and Henry Creswicke Rawlinson. The carved reliefs were found at Sennacherib's immense royal palace of 70 rooms, and discovered specifically inside Room XXXVI, the South-West palace and central room. The carved panels lined over nearly 10,000 ft (3000 m) of the walls, and were 16.7 ft tall (5.10 metres) and 39 ft wide (12 metres). The huge size of these panels, and being hung in the central room of the palace, indicates the importance King Sennacherib gave to this victory battle over one of Judah's cities.

Lachish was one of the most important cities in the Kingdom of Judah, second only to the capital, Jerusalem. Lachish was heavily fortified with massive walls and ramparts, and served as one of the strongholds guarding the interior of Judean territory to resist enemies trying to reach Jerusalem. Just eight years prior to this battle, the Assyrians had destroyed the calf-worshipping ten-tribe Northern kingdom of Israel in 740 BCE. The records of King Sargon II state that 27,290 Israelites from the ten tribes were deported as slaves to various destinations.

In the fourteenth year of King Hezekiah of Judah, Sennacherib and the Assyrians marched upon Lachish and put the city under siege (2 Kings 18:13,17). The Assyrians ultimate military objective was to reach Jerusalem to capture and conquer it.

The Judean soldiers at Lachish put up a hard, valiant fight, but the Assyrians prevailed and took the city. Sennacherib was jubilant and overjoyed at the success of his mission thus far. Being led into exile, the captured Judean soldiers, families, and their household goods and livestock were led out the entrance of the city in a procession past Sennacherib, as he sat in observance, his royal tent stationed behind him. Yes, Sennacherib was personally present on this military campaign. The inscription of the relief says:

> "Sennacherib, king of the world, king of Assyria, sat upon a nimedu-throne before (the city) and passed in review the booty from Lachish."

During the siege of Lachish, Sennacherib had sent a committee of military chiefs to King Hezekiah at Jerusalem to demand surrender. The spokesman was Rabshakeh, who spoke Hebrew fluently. Hezekiah offered to buy Sennacherib off with a heavy tribute of three hundred silver talents and thirty gold talents. However, despite this payment, Rabshakeh and the military chiefs continued to stand outside Jerusalem's walls demanding surrender, even mocking the Most High Yehovah, that even He would not save them. Hezekiah prayed to the Most High, and sent his counselors to the prophet Isaiah to inquire his advice. Yehovah inspired Isaiah to reply, saying that Sennacherib would not enter Judah, but that he would hear a report that will make him return to his land.

Soon thereafter, Rabshakeh pulled away after hearing that Sennacherib had departed Lachish and was fighting in Libnah against Tirhakah the king of Ethiopia, who had come out to fight Sennacherib (2 Kings 19:8,9). According to archaeologist Rawlinson, the Ethiopian and Egyptian army forces of Tirhakah were put to death at Libnah. However, according to Sennacherib's account from the Sennacherib Prism (called Taylor Prism at the British Museum), he states that the Ethiopians and Egyptian armies were defeated "upon the plain of Eltekeh." Eltekeh was an Israelite city of the tribe of Dan, found in the Coastal Plain southeast of Joppa. (Joshua 19:43-46) The inscription on Sennacherib's Prism went on to state:

> "As to Hezekiah the Jew…he did not submit to my yoke, I laid siege to 46 of his strong cities, walled forts and to the countless small villages in their vicinity."

Yet, Sennacherib was unsuccessful in conquering the city of Jerusalem, nor the Kingdom of Judah. After Hezekiah had prayed for deliverance, that night one angel of Yehovah killed 185,000 Assyrian soldiers. When the king of Assyria heard that report, he returned back to his land, just as the prophet Isaiah had prophesied. (2 Kings 19:5-7)

Some modern-day researchers have argued that the captured male prisoners of African descent, as shown in the Lachish reliefs, were not Jews. This is unfortunate, as this should not even be a point of controversy. Here are four very strong reasons that those prisoners were both Hamitic and Jews:

1. Professor Edward H. Plumtre, committee member on the Revised Version of the King James Bible, accepted that the male prisoners were Hamitic, saying in 1881:

"It is significant that the captives are for the most part represented as having woolly hair, as though they had belonged to the Ethiopian army of Tirhakah." The only correction here is that the men captives were not part of Tirhakah's army, nor was Tirhakah's army a part of the battle at Lachish; They were involved in a separate battle at Libnah, which is consistent with 1 Kings 19:8; with archaeologist Henry C. Rawlinson; and with Sennacherib's Prism, which says Tirhakah's defeat ended – not at Lacshish – but in the plain Eltekeh.

2. Ancient Ethiopians and Egyptians did not wear beards. *The Cyclopedia of Biblical, Theological, and Ecclesiastical Literature,* published in 1880, said: "Hence, when Pharaoh sent to summon Joseph from his dungeon, we find it recorded that the patriarch "shaved himself" (Ge 41:14). Shaving was therefore a remarkable custom of the Egyptians." The Jewish Virtual Library says: "the Hittites, Ethiopians, and Sea Peoples are portrayed as clean-shaven." Herodotus also stated: "Egyptians are shaven at other times, *but after a death* they let their hair and beard grow."

In contrast, the ancient Jews were commanded *not to shave off their beards,* according to the Law Covenant. (Leviticus 19:27; 21:5)

3. The Assyrian artisans who were commissioned to carve the panels for Sennacherib's royal palace were very detailed in the events that occurred at the siege of Lachish. Take note: Of all the valuable booty taken from Lachish, what does one notice are the very first images

the artist carved that are being presented before King Sennacherib, as depicted in the relief? They are the male prisoners with the wooly hair. Why did the artist do that? Because the men were Jews, captured from one of the most important cities in the Kingdom of Judah, second only to the capital, Jerusalem. These captured men, no doubt Judean soldiers, were of the Kingdom of Judah, as also were the women and children. Sennacherib was unable to boast and create a relief depicting the capture of Jerusalem, the capital of the Kingdom of Judah. So he chose to instead, boast about the conquest of the second most important city of Judah.

4. The British Museum in London, and the Israel Museum in Jerusalem, both make mention that the people depicted in the reliefs were all Jews. Archaeologist Austin Henry Layard, the person who discovered the Assyrian reliefs, in his book published in 1853, contains a similar artist-drawing of the women and men prisoners from the relief that he saw with his own eyes. Of this drawing, he too, says they are "Jewish Captives from Lachish."

Ancient Lachish has been identified today as an Israeli national park. The park was established on lands of a depopulated Palestinian village called Qobebet Ibn Awwad.

(See Notes)

Black Hebrews Lachish, prisoners taken from Tribe of Judah, 732 BCE.
British Museum, London

Lachish, prisoners taken from Tribe of Judah, 732 BCE.
British Museum, London

Photos | 115

Black Hebrews before Assyrian king, prisoners taken from Tribe of Judah by Assyrian King Sennacherib, 732 BCE. British Museum, London

Relief of Lachish, prisoners taken from Tribe of Judah, 732 BCE. British Museum, London

CHAPTER 10

How the Hebrew Scrolls Foretold the Coming Mashiach

There is nothing more important, more urgent, more purposeful, than to embrace and understand the progressive out-workings of the Most High Yehovah's expressed will and purpose. One major way this can be demonstrated is by understanding the many prophecies recorded in the Tanakh, the Hebrew scriptures, especially those in the Ketuvim, that shed more knowledge on the prophecy in Eden regarding the coming Seed of Judah, Ha-Mashiach (the Messiah).

One of the writings in the Ketuvim that has revealed key essential understanding about Ha-Mashiach is the prophetic Book of Daniel, which describe *three* major "Comings" of the Messiah, whom every person on earth now living at this very hour need to know and act upon.

The following texts will cover the Messiah's first Coming. In Chapter 15 will reveal his Second Coming, or *Parousia*. The events that will occur during his third "Coming" will be covered in the final chapter.

At Daniel 9:20-23, we read Daniel describing how the angel Gabriel came to him to deliver a vision about the coming Messiah:

> "While I was still speaking and praying and confessing my sin and the sin of my people Israel and making my

request for favor before Yehovah my God concerning the holy mountain of my God, yes, while I was yet speaking in prayer, the man Gabriel, whom I had previously seen in the vision, came to me when I was extremely weary at about the time of the evening gift offering.

And he gave me understanding, saying: "O Daniel, now I have come to give you insight and understanding. When you began your entreaty the word went out, and I have come to report it to you, because you are someone very precious. So consider the matter and understand the vision."

The vision Gabriel gave to Daniel is stated in Daniel 9:24-27. Let us now breakdown its key points:

Daniel 9:24: "**Seventy weeks** are decreed upon thy people and upon thy holy city, to make an end of sin, and to forgive iniquity, and to bring in everlasting righteousness, and to seal vision and prophet, and to anoint the Holy of Holies."

We notice a time period of ***Seventy weeks*** are decreed upon Daniel's people, the Hebrew Jews. What is the purpose of the time period? "To make an end of sin, and to forgive iniquity, and to bring in everlasting righteousness." Similar to how the Most High had decreed *70 years* upon His people to be in captivity to Babylon, and then *after those years had expired* the Jews were then released from Babylon's bondage, *so too, after Seventy weeks*, there would be *an end of their sins and everlasting righteousness would be brought in.*

"And to seal vision and prophet." In other words, the fulfillment of Daniel's vision concerning the Messiah would confirm all of the Most High's promises and prophecies.

Was the Seventy weeks in this vision to be understood as meaning *literal* weeks? Let us continue.

> Daniel 9:25: "From the going forth of the word to restore and to build Jerusalem until Messiah, there will be seven weeks, also sixty-two weeks. Jerusalem will return and be actually rebuilt, with a public square and moat, but in the straits of the times."

"From the going forth of the word to restore and to build Jerusalem." This part of the vision was fulfilled in the 20th year of King Artaxerxes of Persia, when the king gave Nehemiah permission to *restore and to build Jerusalem*, as recorded in Nehemiah 2: 1-8. The 20th year of King Artaxerxes was in 455 BCE, and upon his arrival, Nehemiah began rebuilding the walls of Jerusalem between the months of Ab and Elul of that year (Nehemiah 2:17-20; 6:15). The Jewish months of Ab and Elul correspond to July/August, and August/September. We recall that Jerusalem, and the temple, had been destroyed by Nebuchadnezzar of Babylon in 607 BCE. Some of the Jews had returned to Jerusalem with Zerubbabel in 537 BCE to begin rebuilding. But the work was not completed.

"there will be seven weeks." This is referring to the time period of completing the restoration of the city Jerusalem.

"also sixty-two weeks." This is relating to the time period *after* the completion of the city until the coming of the Messiah.

So according to the vision given to Daniel, the Seventy weeks were divided into three periods: (1) seven weeks, (2) sixty-two weeks, and (3) one week, all adding up to "Seventy weeks."

Was Jerusalem and the temple rebuilt in seven literal weeks? No. It took about twenty-one years alone just to complete the temple (Ezra 3:8-10; Ezra 6:13-15). So this vision is not referring to literal weeks, it is referring to prophetic weeks. The angel Gabriel did not mention days in the vision, so these are not weeks of seven days each. *These are weeks of years.* The Most High put the vision in prophetic code. *Each week is seven years long.* Notice Daniel 9:24 in the *American Translation* and the *Revised English Bible*:

> "Seventy weeks of years are destined for your people and for your holy city."

> "Seventy times seven years are marked out for your people and your holy city."

So the "Seventy weeks" mean prophetic years. When do they begin? Daniel 9:25 stated: "From the going forth of the word to restore and to build Jerusalem." Thus, the Seventy weeks began in the year 455 BCE during the 20th year of King Artaxerxes of Persia, when Nehemiah began rebuilding the walls of Jerusalem, between the months of Ab and Elul of that year. The "seven weeks, also sixty-two weeks" is prophetic of *483 years*. Therefore, counting 483 years from 455 BCE would end in the year of 29 CE.

> Daniel 9:26: "And after the sixty-two weeks, Messiah will be cut off, with nothing for himself. And the people of a leader that is coming will destroy the city and the holy place."

This text reveals that the "holy place" – the temple – would be destroyed again. However, the Messiah will be "cut off" – he will die – *before* the destruction of the second temple.

Daniel 9:27: "And he must keep the covenant in force for the many for one week; and at the half of the week he will cause sacrifice and gift offering to cease."

We will discuss the key points of this text shortly. But beforehand, let us examine further the "seven weeks, also sixty-two weeks" that make up the prophetic code of 483 years, which started in 455 BCE during the months Ab-Elul and end in 29 CE.

In one of the books of the Gospels – the Book of Luke – written between 56-58 CE in Greek by a physician, recorded this:

> "In the 15th year of the reign of Tiberius Caesar, when Pontius Pilate was governor of Judea, Herod was district ruler of Galilee, Philip his brother was district ruler of the country of Ituraea and Trachonitis, and Lysanias was district ruler of Abilene, in the days of chief priest Annas and of Caiaphas, God's declaration came to John the son of Zechariah in the wilderness…Now the people were in expectation and all of them were reasoning in their hearts about John, "May he perhaps be the Christ?" (Luke 3:1, 15)

The people in Palestine at that time were in expectation of *the Christ*, which is the Greek word for *Messiah* in Hebrew. So in effect, the people were reasoning, "May he perhaps be the Messiah?" The people knew for years the prophecy of Daniel about the Seventy weeks, so that is why they were in expectation. They knew the time for the appearance of the Messiah was approaching near. Many thought that perhaps John the baptist was the "Anointed One." However, there is something else in this text passage that must not be missed.

The writer and physician Luke stated that these events were happening, "In the 15th year of the reign of Tiberius Caesar."

Tiberius Caesar was named Roman Emperor by the Roman Senate in September, 14 CE, after Gaius Octavius, or better known as Caesar Augustus, died on August 19, 14 CE. This is all confirmed by ancient historian Suetonius, as well as the official Roman Fasti (Calendar). (See Notes) Why is this important? The writer Luke continues:

> "John gave the answer, saying to all: "I, for my part, baptize you with water, but the one stronger than I am is coming, the lace of whose sandals I am not worthy to untie. He will baptize you with holy spirit and with fire…Now when all the people were baptized, Yeshua too was baptized."

Luke reports that a person named Yeshua was baptized by John the Baptist, in the 15th year of the reign of Tiberius Caesar. Another writer, Matthew, who was a tax collector, wrote an account in 40 CE of this same event, which also became part of the gospels:

> "In those days John the Baptist came preaching in the wilderness of Judea…Then Yeshua came from Galilee to the Jordan to John, in order to be baptized by him…after being baptized, Yeshua immediately came up from the water." (Matthew 3:1,13,16)

Regarding Yeshua, both accounts by Luke and Matthew stated that Yeshua's parents were Joseph and Mary of Nazareth, who were both members of the tribe of Judah, and both descendants of King David, according to the Jewish genealogical rolls that were available at that time. (See Notes) So what was the 15th year of Tiberius Caesar's reign? Since he was confirmed by the Roman Senate in September, 14 CE, his 15th year would have been around September, 29 CE.

According to the vision given to Daniel, Ha-Mashiach would appear when the "seven weeks, also sixty-two weeks" ended, which began counting for 483 years starting in 455 BCE around the months of Ab/Elul when Nehemiah completed the walls of Jerusalem, and thus, would end in the year of 29 CE.

Yeshua was baptized in the autumn of 29 CE, in the 15th year of the reign of Tiberius Caesar.

Coincidence?

The Most High said that there will be those "Who have eyes but do not see, and ears but do not hear." (Isaiah 6:9,10)

Let us examine the last part of Daniel's vision:

Daniel 9:27: "And he must keep the covenant in force for the many for one week; and at the half of the week he will cause sacrifice and gift offering to cease."

Here we come down to the last week of the vision, the "one week", which, when added to the other weeks, makes the "Seventy weeks" in total. As has already been established, these are prophetic weeks. So, to be consistent, in this prophecy the "one week" is actually, not seven days, but are *7 years*. And, the vision states that "He" the Messiah, "will cause sacrifice and gift offering to cease" *at the half of the week."* Let us examine this final part of the vision in relation to Yeshua, the one who was baptized in the Jordan river in the autumn of 29 CE.

At Luke 4, verses 1 and 2, it states that after Yeshua was baptized he went to the wilderness for 40 days. This would have been September going into October 29 CE.

Using another book of the gospels as a historical reference point, the account of the fisherman John, let us see what it reveals how many times Yeshua attended the annual Passover in Jerusalem. The Passover was celebrated annually on Nisan 14 after sundown.

> John 2:13: "Now the Passover of the Jews was near, and Yeshua went up to Jerusalem" This was Passover of 30 CE.

> John 5:1: "After this there was a festival of the Jews, and Yeshua went up to Jerusalem." This was Passover of 31 CE

> John 6:3,4: "So Yeshua went up on a mountain and sat down there with his disciples. Now the Passover, the festival of the Jews, was near." This was Passover 32 CE

> John 12:1: "Six days before the Passover, Yeshua arrived at Bethany."

> John 13:2: "Now because he knew before the festival of the Passover that his hour had come for him to leave this world and go to the Father…the evening meal was going on." This was the evening of Passover 33 CE.

In 33 CE, that date would have corresponded to our April 3rd. The months of the Jews generally ran from the middle of the month to the middle of the next month. If one examines the Passovers that Yeshua attended according to the accounts in the Book of John, we notice that Yeshua attended the annual Passover between a period of three years and six months:

> 1 year: The autumn of 29 CE to October 30 CE

> 2nd year: The autumn of 30 CE to October 31 CE

> 3rd year: The autumn of 31 CE to October 32 CE

Six Months: October 32, November 32, December 32, January 33, February 33, and then the sixth month, March, which ran from mid-March to mid April 33 CE.

Daniel 9:27: "And he must keep the covenant in force for the many for one week; and *at the half of the week* he will cause sacrifice and gift offering to cease." The prophetic "half of the week" meant 3 years and six months.

Yeshua was hung on a stake (not a cross) on Passover, Nisan 14, 33 CE

Coincidence?

According to the Gospel accounts, Yeshua stated on many occasions that he was the son of the Most High, and was sent by Him to give his life as a guilt offering for many and to carry the sins of the people. (See Isaiah 53) Was he the foretold Coming Seed of Judah?

What other ancient historical sources, outside biblical texts, mention the events of Yeshua's life?

CHAPTER 11

Historical Evidentiary Support Yeshua Is Foretold Messiah

Here are historical sources, outside the Bible, which speak of a man known as Jesus Christ as a historical person whom people in the 1st Century CE either saw, spoke to, referenced, or heard verifiable reports about.

Spoiler: These are strong evidentiary sources. You be the Judge.

- "When, therefore, Ananus was of this disposition, he thought he had now a proper opportunity…so he convened the judges of the Sanhedrin and brought before them a man named James, **the brother of Jesus who was called the Christ**, and certain others." Josephus, *Antiquities of the Jews*, Book 20, Chapter 9

- "Chritus, the founder of the name, had undergone the death penalty in the reign of Tiberius, by sentence of the procurator Pontius Pilate, and the pernicious superstition was checked for a moment, only to break out once more, not only in Judaea, the first source of the evil, but even in Rome." Tacitus, *Annals*, Book 15, Chapter 44. Written circa 116 CE. (Chritus was the Latin word for Christ)

- "On the eve of Passover Yeshu the Nazarean was hanged." Gemara, Babylonia Talmud, Sanhedrin 43a, Munich Codex. The oldest known complete manuscript of the Babylonian Talmud. The Munich Codex is also known as Hebrew Manuscript 95. 9th Century CE. (Yeshu was the Aramaic word for Yeshua)

- "And the women also, which came with him from Galilee, followed after, and beheld the sepulchre, and how his body was laid. And they returned, and prepared spices and ointments…Now upon the first day of the week, very early in the morning, they came…bringing the spices they had prepared…And they entered in, and found not the body of the Lord Jesus. And it came to pass, as they were much perplexed thereabout, behold, two men stood by them in shining garments…He is not here, but is risen… And returned from the sepulchre, and told all these things unto the eleven, and to all the rest. It was Mary Magdalene, and Joanna, and Mary the mother of James, and other women that had been with them, which told these things unto the apostles. ***And their words seemed to them as idle tales, and they believed them not.***" (Luke 23:55-24:1-11) According to the Bible, it was the women who were the first to learn that Yeshua had risen from the dead. In ancient Palestine, women were looked down upon. The testimony of a woman was considered equal to that of a slave. It is no surprise, then, that the apostles did not believe the women, in view of the prevailing attitude toward women at that time. Being imperfect, the apostles still had things to work on. Today, many believe the Greek Scriptures of the Bible were invented. So then, why would Luke record that Yeshua's resurrection was first discovered by women if this really did not happen? Why would these details be invented back then, which would portray the men in an unfavorable and embarrassing light if it did not happen? The account only makes sense if it was true.

- In Justin Martyr's work *Dialogue with Trypho,* written between 155-160 CE, he mentions that certain Jews were saying that *the body of Jesus was stolen from the tomb by his disciples.* There is no contemporary written record found anywhere that refuted Martyr's statement. It was a common belief, which he was merely echoing at the time. ***But this statement could not have been said if the tomb was <u>Not</u> empty. If it was common knowledge that Jesus' body was still in the tomb, then why would a belief that the body was stolen still persist?*** Martyr would have been making himself look foolish! So the tomb *was* empty. ***Yeshua's body was not there***. Chapter 108

- According to official Roman governor reports written by Pontius Pilate, he stated that Yeshua was nailed in both his hands and feet, **and had performed miracles to heal diseases and raise the dead**. *The Acts of Pontius Pilate*, mentioned in *First Apology of Justin Martyr*, Chapters 35 & 48. Written between 155-157 CE.

(See Notes)

CHAPTER 12

Christendom's Conspiracy to Enslave Descendants of the Seed

Throughout recorded history, the Most High has revealed His expressed will regarding the Hebrew Jews, who were used multiple times in fulfilling His timely prophecies. The Hebrew Jews experienced many times the day of Jubilee and the mornings of a joyful cry. But there were also many dark nights of trials and tribulations. And they had many enemies who wished to extinguish them. In fact, it could be argued that the curse upon the Hebrew Jews was perhaps worse than the curse of Canaan, who's curse lasted up through the time of the Roman empire, and possibly still in effect today. Even the Benjamite Paul in the Bible, who was mistaken for being one of the Egyptian dagger-men, prophesied about a coming satanic enemy, who would attempt to destroy All of the Most High Yehovah's people, right down to the last days of this world. Will the Most High make a way out for His people during the dangerous dark days ahead?

Let us briefly review certain historical timelines involving the Hebrew Jews, and then examine a prophetic warning that the Most High moved Benjamite Paul the apostle to record.

It was Abraham who crossed the Euphrates River and sojourned into the Land of Canaan many millenniums ago in the year 1943

BCE, and while there was met by the high priest Melchizedek, the King of Salem, that is, Jeru-Salem. During this journey, the covenant between Yehovah and Abraham went into effect, that, "Through your seed, all the families of the earth will be Blessed."

Hundreds of years later, the Ephramite Joshua and the army of Israel entered Canaan, which means Merchant Land; Land of the Tradesman. The city of Gaza formed a land bridge which connected Egypt, who exercised suzerainty over the Canaan region. Although the Canaanites were known as tradesmen, they also were known for their worship of Baal, which included idolatry, gross sexual depravity, spiritism, and child sacrifice. During the wars of the Most High, the Canaanite kings were defeated by Israel, and the land was cleansed of its unclean practices, whereupon the land began to be known by its new name, Judea.

Over time, the Canaanites and Israelites were able to peacefully co-exist within Judea. Thus, we have the gospel account of when Yeshua performed a miracle for a Canaanite woman (Phoenicians were Canaanites in origin). However, by 70 CE, history recounts the destruction of Jerusalem and its temple by the Roman armies, and Hebrew Jews were scattered to North Africa and other parts of the Roman Empire, just as they were in 607, 732, and 740 BCE to Media, Babylon, Upper Euphrates, Persia, Iraq, Ethiopia, and wherever else. In 70 CE, 97,000 Jews were sold into slavery. Yeshua had said, "Jerusalem will be trampled on by the Gentiles until the times of the Gentiles are fulfilled." After the second Jewish revolt between 132-135 CE, the Jews were scattered, killed, and sold again into slavery, and the Romans banned them from entering the city of Jerusalem for nearly two centuries. The province of Judea was renamed *Syria Palaestina* in an attempt to get rid of the name Judea. The Hebrews who believed that Yeshua was the Messiah were also scattered.

This brief overview from Abraham to the birth of Syria Palestine brings us now to the main part of this discussion. As was stated earlier, Paul the apostle, whose knowledge about the Law Covenant made him follow Yeshua, was inspired by the Most High to record these words about a coming Enemy:

> "Let no one seduce you in any manner because it will not come unless the apostasy comes first and the man of lawlessness gets revealed, the son of destruction…the lawless one's presence is according to the operation of Satan with every powerful work and lying signs and portents"

When would this "Man of lawlessness" come?

In 325 CE, Roman Emperor Constantine the Great presided over the Council of Nicaea, a convening of "apostate Christian" bishops in all the realm of Christendom, in order to reach consensus on various apostate church doctrine and canon law set up by man, not by the Most High. Nor was it set up by Yeshua, or by any of his apostles, even though the council uses Christ's name. This council was a precursor to the Catholic popes of the Holy Roman Empire.

At the end of the council, it had been decided that Rome should not celebrate their festival of Easter on the same date as the Jewish Passover because:

> "…it appeared an unworthy thing that in the celebration of this most holy feast we should follow the practice of the Jews."

Constantine himself expresses the decision this way:

> "It was, in the first place, declared improper to follow the custom of the Jews in the celebration of this holy festival,

because, their hands having been stained with crime…Let us, then have nothing in common with the Jews, who are our adversaries…avoiding all contact with that evil way"

The Roman festival of Easter is pagan in of itself. As to its origin, the name Easter comes from the Chaldean goddess of fertility whose name was Astarte. It should be added that Yeshua, nor his apostles, ever promote Easter in any way, shape, or form. Yeshua celebrated the Passover. The Gospels state that after he had concluded the Passover meal on the night of his arrest, he then instituted a new & simple observance – the passing of bread and wine – in symbol of his blood and body, which he would sacrifice for the Hebrew people, and for anyone – leaving instructions that this be done every Passover "in remembrance of me."

The Council of Nicaea also introduced the foundation for the false teaching of the Trinity (three gods in one), another pagan teaching from ancient Babylon, which Yeshua or his apostles never taught, nor is taught in the Bible. Yeshua never believed in the Trinity doctrine. Yeshua said,"Hear O Israel, Yehovah your God is one Yehovah," quoting from Deuteronomy 6:4. For this very reason, Paul gave the warning that "from among you men will rise and speak twisted things to draw away the disciples after themselves." Many other pagan teachings crept into the church, including hellfire, Christmas, and the Cross. Alexander Hislop, in his book *The Two Babylons,* explained regarding the Cross:

> "In Egypt the earliest form of that which has since been *called* the cross, was no other than the "Crux Ansata", or "Sign of life" borne by Osiris and all the Egyptian gods; that the *ansa* or "handle" was afterwards dispensed with, and that it became the simple Tau, or ordinary cross, as it appears at

this day…but was simply the result of the attachment to old and long-cherished Pagan symbols, which is always strong in those who, with the adoption of the Christian name and profession, are still, to a large extent, Pagan in heart and feeling. This, and only this, is the origin of the worship of the "cross."

In 329 CE, Constantine issued laws prohibiting Jews to own "Christian" slaves, punishable by death conversion of "Christians" to Judaism, and forbidding to perform circumcision on slaves. Another law was passed prohibiting marriage between Jews and "Christians."

In 411 CE, the Germanic tribe of the Visigoths of Gaul moved into Iberia, a Roman province, and took possession of it. This Roman province, originally called *Hispania Ulterior*, was a place for retired military who had fought for Rome, starting with Augustus. Emperor Marcus Salvius Otho was once the governor of this province in 58/59 BCE. The province had a golden statue of Emperor Titus who, as general during the Jewish revolt in 70 CE, had sent 97,000 Hebrew Jews into slavery. Some of those Jewish slaves may have been sent to the province of Hispania.

The Visigoths ruled Iberia for the next 300 years. Some Jews, who had already scattered to Iberia or migrated there from Syria Palestine prior, would soon face severe edicts. Between 589-694, several edicts against Jews were passed by the Visigoth's Council of Toledo:

589 CE – Forcibly baptizing children of mixed Jewish/Catholic marriages; Forbidden from holding public office.

613 CE – Jews to be expelled or convert to the Catholic Church; As many as 90,000 converted; Some fled to North

Africa and intermingled with the Berber tribes, converting many of them and intermarriage.

633 CE – Catholics practicing Judaism secretly were to have their children taken away from them.

653 CE – Forbidden to practice Jewish worship; Anyone discovered to have aided Jews in their worship shall face seizure of one fourth of their property and excommunication.

694 CE – Visigoth King Egica learned of an alleged plot between Jews in Iberia and North Africa who were collaborating with the Moors for an invasion; Declared all Jews to be made slaves and their masters to insure their slaves not observe Jewish customs; These measures were only partly implemented.

On April 30, 711 CE, an army of 7000 Berbers under the Moor Tariq ibn Ziyad landed at Gibraltar, followed by Arab Muslim soldiers, which led to eventual Muslim rule of Southern Iberia. The persecution of Jews under the Visigoths ended with the Moor/Arab conquest (Note: There was a rare outburst of violence in 1066 when a Jewish vizier for the Berber King of Granada was killed in a plot to betray the kingdom; Sadly, it resulted in a massacre of 1,500 Jewish households by Muslims).

In 1095, the Papacy proclaimed the Crusades on Muslims, in response to Muslim control of Jerusalem. These Crusades lasted from 1095-1291. They were, however, unsuccessful. The Papacy authorized a Crusade in 1147 for the Iberia Peninsula against the Moors, resulting in the Moors losing Lisbon, Cordoba, and Algarve, leaving the Emirate of Granada as the last Muslim state on the Iberia Peninsula

Christendom's Conspiracy to Enslave Descendants of the Seed | 137

by 1249. Scattered wars and skirmishes would continue taking place between Christendom and Muslims for the next two hundred years.

But something different was about to occur towards the mid-1400's. What would the Roman Papacy plot and conspire to do?

Conspiring first with Portugal, and later with Spain, the Papacy of the Holy Roman Empire of Christendom schemed a plan: "With due meditation" the Papacy would "by letters of ours" grant King Afonso V of Portugal to capture "Guineamen and other Negroes taken by force and subdue all" enemies of Christendom, and "to reduce them to perpetual slavery."

Staring from 1441, a blitzkrieg to colonize the West Coast of Africa was underway. Slave raids and slave ports began being set up from Arguin Bay to Senegal between 1443-1455.

Here is the entire edict, or papal bull, of January 8, 1455:

> "And so it came to pass that when a number of ships of this kind had explored and taken possession of very many harbors, islands, and seas, that at length came to **the province of Guinea**, and having taken possession of some islands and harbors and the sea adjacent to that province, sailing father they came to the mouth of a certain great river commonly supposed to be the Nile, **and war was waged for some years against the peoples of those parts** in the name of the said King Alfonso…Thence also **many Guineamen and other Negroes, taken by force**, and some by barter of unprohibited articles, or by other lawful contract of purchase, have been sent to the said kingdoms…**We weighing all and singular the premises with due meditation**, and noting that since we had formerly **by other letters of ours granted** among other things free and ample faculty to the aforesaid King Alfonso

– to invade, search out, capture, vanquish, and subdue all Saracens and pagans whatsoever, and other enemies of Christ wheresoever placed, and the kingdoms, dukedoms, principalities, dominions, possessions, and all movable and immovable goods whatsoever held and possessed by them **and to reduce their persons to perpetual slavery,** and to apply and appropriate to himself and his successors the kingdoms, dukedoms, counties, principalities, dominions, possessions, and goods, and to convert them to his and their use and profit…"

By the mid-1450's, the slave trading stations at Arguin and Senegal were estimated by slave trader Alvise Cadamosto to have brought 700-800 African slaves annually to Portugal from down the Senegal River, which was called the "Western Nile" mistakenly at that time. Portugal, and later Spain, the puppets of the Papacy, were also intent to locate and secure gold.

By the backing and power handed from the Papacy, another slave-trading post was set up, called *El Mina*, in Accra, Ghana in 1482. Ten years later, the Emirate of Granada was taken over by Spain in January 1492. Three months later, the Alhambra Decree was passed, giving the Jews four months, July 31, to either convert to the Catholic Church or be expelled. The exact number expelled is unknown, as some estimate 40,000, while others estimate 100,000 Jews. Many fled to Africa, while others to the Ottoman Empire and Italy. But the worst was not over. The Papacy issued two papal bulls on May 3, 1493, granting Spain the same permissions and favors in West Africa as was Portugal. King Ferdinand sent instructions to his colonial governor in Haiti:

"Because with great care we have procured the conversion of the Indians to our Holy Catholic Faith, and furthermore, if there are still people there who are doubtful of the faith in their own conversions, it would be a hindrance, and therefore we will not permit, nor allow to go there Moors, nor Jews nor heretics nor reconciled heretics, nor persons who are recently converted to our faith, **except if they are negro slaves, or other slaves**, that have been born under the dominion of our natural Christian subjects." (September 16, 1501)

In other words, no free Moors or free Jews would be sent to Haiti; except if they are *Negro slaves, or other slaves*. Just as slavery was foretold in Deuteronomy 28, notice how it through the Most High's servant John in Revelation chapter 18:

*"One of the seven angels who had the seven bowls came and said to me: Come, I will show you the judgment on the great prostitute who sits on many waters…**Babylon the Great**…a full cargo of gold, silver, precious stones, pearls…cattle, sheep, horses, carriages, **slaves, and human beings**…and every ship captain and every man that voyages anywhere, and sailors and all those who make a living by the sea, stood at a distance"*

Is there evidence that Black Jewish slaves were sent to America? This will be explored in Chapter 14. The next chapter, however, must also not be left out: Specifically, the *real reason* for Christopher Columbus' third voyage to the Americas.

Astarte, Babylon-Chaldean pagan goddess of fertility. Known today as Easter.

Photos | 141

Ancient Cross. Its pagan origins are from Babylon-Chaldea.

Tiberius Caesar. The fifteenth year of his reign was 29 CE, the end of the "69 weeks." That same year Yeshua was baptized by John the baptist.

Justin Martyr. In his work "Dialogue with Trypho", Justin Martyr speaks of persistent rumors in his day that Jesus' body was stolen by his disciples. Apparently the body was not in the tomb on the third day.

Pontius Pilate. He is quoted from his own official records, called "Acts of Pontius Pilate" in Justin Martyr's works, where Pilate went on record stating that "Jesus" performed miracles and raised the dead.

CHAPTER 13

The Real Reason Columbus Took His Third Voyage

In Christopher Columbus' journal regarding his third voyage to the Americas in 1498, he made some very, very interesting statements, statements that need to be reviewed again, because they need to be made crystal clear in this journey for truth, or in this case, for historical truth. First off – we are NOT referring to the report of, "there had come to Española from the south and south-east, a black people who have the tops of their spears made of a metal which they call guanin, of which he had sent samples to the Sovereigns to have them assayed, when it was found that of 32 parts, 18 were of gold, 6 of silver and 8 of copper."

No, we are not embarking on a re-examining of that very well known reference which is quoted, right-fully so, as evidence of a pre-Columbus, pre-European arrival to the Americas by African explorers. There is another statement that Columbus made in his journal, which is equally strong, if not stronger evidence, of African contact to the Americas which pre-dates Columbus' trip to South America.

Here is the first part of Columbus' statement on his third voyage that we will breakdown:

| 145

1498

> "He left there Saturday, June 30, at night for the island of Santiago, where he arrived on Sunday at the hour of the vespers, because it is distant 28 leagues: and this is the principal one of the Cape Verdes... The Admiral says again that he wishes to go to the south, because he intends with the aid of the Most Holy Trinity, to find islands and lands, that God may be served and their Highnesses and Christianity may have pleasure, **and that he wishes to see what was the idea of King Don Juan of Portugal**, who said that there was mainland to the south... And the Admiral says further that the said King Don Juan was certain that within those limits famous lands and things must be found..."

Notice Columbus said **that** *"he wishes to see what was the idea of King Don Juan of Portugal, who said that there was mainland to the south."* He is referring to King John II of Portugal. But what was King John's idea that Columbus wished to see? It was a report that King John had received that there was a mainland to the south. What is interesting is that when Columbus headed out on his third voyage, the year was 1498. However, King John II was already dead, since he had died in October 1495. Therefore, King John's "idea" was a report that had come to the King's attention and was discussed with Columbus at least three years previous. What was this report?

> *"And the Admiral says further that the said King Don Juan was certain that within those limits famous lands and things must be found. Certain principal inhabitants of the island of Santiago came to see them, and they said that to the south-west*

of the island of Huego, which is one of the Cape Verde, distant twelve leagues from this, may be seen an island..."

The person writing this account is Columbus' assistant, the Spanish friar and priest Bartolome' de Las Casas, who refers to Columbus as "the Admiral." Who brought this report to King John? Las Casas writes that certain principal inhabitants of Santiago, Cape Verde, had reported they could see an island about 12 leagues away.

Now notice what else was reported to the King:

*"and that the King Don Juan was greatly inclined to send to make discoveries to the south-west and **that canoes had been found which start from the coasts of Guinea and navigate to the west with merchandise."***

These men of Santiago who had brought this report to the king stated that "canoes had been found" which came "from the coasts of Guinea" West Africa, and the canoes had navigated to the west carrying "merchandise." In other words, Africans from the coast of Guinea had sent canoes with trading merchandise to an island 12 leagues west!

This is the *real reason* why Columbus made a third trip to the Americas – **the report suspected that West Africans had already found the island, and were engaging in trade with it!**

Having finally gotten his financial backing of six ships, a crew, and supplies, Columbus was now ready to depart to this island and verify if the King's report was accurate. Notice what happened next:

*"Wednesday, July 4…he ordered the course laid to the way of the south-west, which is the route leading from these islands to the south… **because then he would be on a parallel with the land of the sierra of Loa (Sierra Leone) and cape of Sancta Ana in***

> *Guinea, which is below the equinoctial line, where he says that below that line of the world are found more gold and things of value; and that after, he would navigate, the Lord pleasing, **to the west, and from there would go to this Española, in which route he would prove the theory of the King John aforesaid.**"*

Columbus followed the same sailing route as the West Africans, by sailing south to Sierra Leone, then sailing due west to Trinidad and reaching the top of the island – which was South America:

> *"Tuesday, August 7, there came an infinite number of Indians by land and by sea and all brought with them bread and maize and things to eat and pitchers of beverages…**they brought handkerchiefs of cotton very symmetrically woven and worked in colours like those brought from Guinea, from the rivers of the Sierra Leona and of no difference…below he says that these handkerchiefs resemble 'almayzars'***

> *"But Wednesday, August 8, a canoe came with 12 men to the caravel and they took them all, and brought them to the ship of the Admiral, and from them he chose six and sent the others to land…and those whom he had taken told him there were people who were clothed, for which reason he decided to anchor, and infinite canoes came to the ships. These are his words. **Each one, he says, wore his cloth so woven in colours, that it appeared an 'almayzar,' with one tied on the head and the other covering the rest, as has been already explained.**"*

On August 7, 1498, once he reached the coast of South America, Columbus reported that the indigenous people brought his men cotton handkerchiefs woven in the same symmetrical pattern and colors like those he had seen when he was trading in Guinea at Sierra Leone and El Mina between 1482 and 1485. Columbus called these African cotton headbands *Almayzars*, an Arabic word for wrapper/cover. Just as Van Sertima had pointed out in his research, when Columbus saw the headdresses and loincloths, he now knew that West Africans had already made contact on the continent.

In conclusion, on the isthmus linking Central and South America is the country of Panama. In Panama, lay the province of Darien, partially bordered by Columbia and the Pacific Ocean. This coast, covered by dense forest, are inhabited by a people known as the Darien or San Blas, but also by another name, the indigenous *Mandinga*, who have lived here hundreds of years before the Spaniards came. It was reported that about 3000 Mandinga inhabited the area in 1865, and in 1747, the governor of the province reported about 5000 families. From *whom* did the indigenous Mandinga get their name?

CHAPTER 14

Black Jews Brought to America During Slavery

The Portuguese Crown began meddling with the Kingdom of *Kongo* and the region of west-central Congo around 1483 CE. At first, it was for the purposes of exchanging cultures and trade. Even nobles from the royal court of Kongo and Catholic missionaries from Portugal were exchanged between both kingdoms by 1491. Within the region of the Congo lived nomadic Jews, many who had been pushed out of Egypt-Nubia due to the Muslim conquest of Egypt that had occurred in the 7th Century CE. These "wandering Jews" moved into the Congo to avoid persecution and forced conversion to Islam from the Muslims.

In 1575, the Portuguese had established a colony called Luanda, along the West African coastline, which later became a slave port for Portuguese Angola. (See Notes) Oddly enough, it was during this same time when Italian cosmographer from Venice, Livio Sanuto, was in the Congo working on maps of Africa he hoped to publish for the world to see. In his notes regarding the Congo region, Sanuto had written in Latin, *Iudeorum Terra*, when translated means "Land of the Jews." Sanuto later died in 1576, and his brother Giulio Sanuto eventually published, in 1588, twelve maps of Africa that Livio had completed. On top of that, in 1492, King John of Portugal appointed

Alvaro de Caminha as governor of Saint Thomas island, who took two thousand Black Jewish children of seven years old and under from their parents in former Moorish Granada, because "the Said King Sold all those *Jews* for Slaves that refus'd to embrace the Roman Religion.."

This historical information needs to be understood and linked to the context of the Trans-Atlantic Slave trade to America, and to the Americas. The enslaved who were forcibly brought to Virginia, the Carolinas, and New York were from the Congo region where Black Jews resided! Out of all the millions of enslaved who came to America, would it be logical to conclude that not a single Black Jew was among them? That conclusion would actually be illogical. The enslaved who came to Virginia beginning from 1619, as well as those beginning in 1626 to New York, were slaves from the Congo, the "Land of the Jews."

Another example. One of the largest slave ports in West Africa was called Whydah, or Ouidah, also known as the Slave Coast (in present-day Benin, next to Ghana, known then as the Gold Coast). Vast numbers of enslaved were loaded onto ships from there. However, since the sixteenth Century the Portuguese called that slave port *Ajuda*, because "its inhabitants were said to be Jews" and "considered to be a remnant of scattered tribes of Israel." In fact, Welsh engraver Emanuel Bowen published a map of this area in 1747, describing this slave port by engraving the words, "Km of Juda or Whidah SLAVE COAST." Does no possibility exist that at one of the largest slave ports in West Africa during the slave trade, where a Jewish kingdom or community has been documented, would have even a single enslaved Black Jew among the many slave cargos that hoisted off its shores to America? Professor Godbey pointed out: As persecuted communities, Jewish "Negroes" were more in danger than others of being raided by war-parties and sold as slaves. Godbey went on to say that he considered it *Certain* that many Jewish "Negroes" were among the slaves brought to America and the Americas. Here are some examples:

A large population of black and mulatto Jews began to appear in the 1780's in Suriname and Jamaica. Their descendants are now showing up on DNA genetic testings.

Wentworth Mathews, born about 1892 in the West Indies, came to Manhattan, New York in 1913 and identified himself as a Black Jew. Mathews stated his grandfather was one of the Black Jews of Nigeria, and was carried to St. Christopher in the West Indies, where Mathews and his father were born. Another account also points to such evidence. (See Notes)

Olaudah Equiano was kidnapped in 1756 from his Igbo village of Essaka (in present-day Nigeria) and enslaved in Virginia, England, and the Leeward Islands. In his autobiography, Equiano stated that his Igbo tribe practiced the same customs of the Jews in the Torah. He was able to gain his freedom later in the United States.

Billy Simmons was a Black Jew, born in Madagascar around 1780 and purchased by white Jewish slave owners and brought to Charleston, South Carolina. He attended services at a Jewish synagogue during the 1850's.

A slave named London in Savannah, Georgia, translated the Gospel of John into Gullah using Arabic letters. His birthplace is unknown. He died in Florida, where his slave owner later moved, sometime before 1858. During London's lifetime, it was speculated he was Mandingo. While the word *Mandingos* meant a people from a particular region in West Africa, the word was also a synonym for *African Muslims* in the minds of Southern whites. Although direct evidence that London was a Jew is lacking, his story provides two very important insights into answering the question whether more Black Jews were in America other than the few documented cases currently known.

First, London's story directs one to the language and culture of the Gullah people of the Georgia and South Carolina seaboard. How did the Gullah language originate? The people themselves, who have proudly carried and preserved the history and traditions of their culture for hundreds of years, have stated how the slaves, out of the various African regions from which they came, had to develop a form of communication amongst themselves. Thus, an amalgamation of words and phrases from the respective languages that each enslaved person possessed became, over time, one language, a collective language, their language. Researchers among the Gullah have traced the origin of some of their language words to Sierra Leone. Other researchers point to Angola as another original source.

WHERE DID THE WORD *GULLAH* ITSELF COME FROM?
Surprisingly, the word *Gullah* is found in the Hebrew language. In Hebrew, the word means "REDEEM." (LEVITICUS 25:24, 29, 32, 49)

Interestingly, the spiritual "Kum ba yah" is an African American spiritual known to be sung in the Gullah culture, with ties to enslaved West Africans.

The song was originally an appeal to God to come and help those in need.

There are many who say the phrase means: "COME BY HERE," meaning "PLEASE GOD COME HERE," a cry for help among those enslaved.

According to the book *Sweetgrass Baskets And The Gullah Tradition* by Joyce V. Coakley, the phrase "Bring Em Yuh" is translated "Bring It Here."

Another phrase, "Come Yuh or Been Yuh? can be translated, Have You Come To Visit Here, or You Been Here? In other words - ARE YOU A TOURIST OR RESIDENT?

Consider a few comparisons between Hebrew and Gullah words:

Gullah word *DA* and *DADA*: MOTHER, NURSE, OR ELDERLY WOMAN. (In GHANA & BENIN it means "MOTHER, OR ELDER SISTER)

Hebrew word *DAGAR (DAW-GAR)*: TO BROOD OVER ITS EGGS, IT YOUNG

Hebrew word *DA DAH*: "TO WALK GENTLY, GO SLOWLY"

Gullah word *DAH*: MOTHER, GRANDMOTHER, RELATIVE, CAREGIVER, OR AUNT.

Hebrew word *DOWDAH (DO-DAW)*: A FATHER'S SISTER, AN UNCLE'S WIFE.

Gullah word *DEDE*: CORRECT, EXACT, EXACTLY. (In YORUBA It means the same thing. In the KONGO it means "SIMILARITY")

Hebrew word *DA HEE*: ENOUGH, MORE THAN ENOUGH, MUCH AS IS SUFFICIENT, TOO MUCH.

(EXODUS 36:5,7; DEUTERONOMY 15:8; PROVERBS 25:16)

Gullah word *SWONGUH*: PROUD

Hebrew word *SAW-GAB*: TO BE LOFTY, EXALT, BE EXCELLENT, BE HIGH OR LOFTY, BE TOO STRONG. (ISAIAH 2:11, 17; ISAIAH 12:4; ISAIAH 26:5)

The phrase "Kum Ba Yah" may also have another meaning. In the Gullah language, the title *Buh* or *Bah* is often added in front of a man's name to denote honor and kinship. So the spiritual "Kum Ba Yah" might actually be translated, "Come Great And Honorable Yah," since the word *Yah* in Hebrew is a shortened word for the Most High's personal name in scripture.

Therefore, since Gullah is based on different varieties of words from languages in Africa, could not then Hebrew have found its way into some word phrases of the Gullah language? Hebrew was also a language spoken in Africa, and especially among Black Jews. Of course, we can expect there to be slight variations in accent and spelling. (See Notes)

Another insight we can learn from the account about the slave London is the fact that he knew Arabic, which many enslaved persons in America knew. In fact, there are far more documented accounts of enslaved persons in America speaking Arabic than there are of those who were Jewish, let alone speaking Hebrew (there is documented case of an African slave church in Savannah, GA). This brings us to an additional aspect of Arabic-speaking slaves that most often is completely overlooked in the discussion of Black Jews: **Many Black Jews had converted to Islam, and/or identified as Muslim before they arrived in America.** There are many accounts of nomadic Black Jews in Africa who were either fleeing persecution from Muslims and fending off pressure to convert to Islam, or trying to maintain their Hebrew identity from assimilation into pagan-fetish tribes. Some Jews were successful in retaining their Judaic heritage. But others were unsuccessful. Over time, their Hebrew identity became lost, their descendants still observing pieces of their former customs and laws, but not understanding why. *They arrived in America as enslaved Jews, but no longer knew they were Jews. They came speaking Arabic and identified as Muslim.* Any semblance of a memory some still had remaining of their Hebrew Israelite identity, would fade out as more trauma & persecution from the plantation slave owner sank in. Now, even retaining Arabic would prove a challenge, let alone Hebrew or an Ethiopian language, unless in remote slave communities like the Gullah.

This must be the reason why there are so few accounts found in America of Black Hebrew Jews *who identified as such.*

Here is another account – of Omar ibn Said, a man enslaved in North Carolina, whose account will be examined now.

Omar ibn Said was born about 1770 in his birthplace of Futa Toro, a Fulani district in Senegal. He identified himself as Fula and Muslim. As his autobiographical narrative in Arabic states, Omar was raised as a Mohammedan, learned Arabic, and in time taught Arabic and the prayers as a young man in his country. Omar became a dealer in cotton cloths. But one day around 1807, "there came to our place a large army who killed many men, and took me, and brought me to the great sea, and sold me," whereupon he was bound and put on a slave ship that landed in Charleston, South Carolina. Omar was sold to a slave owner, but escaped, ran away, and eventually was caught. While in jail, Omar began writing Arabic on the walls of the jail from coals he found in some ashes. He was sold to a slave holder named General Owens of Bladen County, North Carolina and spent the rest of his life there. The account includes a statement that the Owens family later in life gave Omar a copy of the Koran and the Bible, both in Arabic.

Omar ibn Said stated his birthplace was among the Fulani, or Fulas. Had the Fulas originally been Jews before they became Muslim? The book, *The Lost Tribes A Myth,* by Allen Godbey (1930), states that the Fulani have a tradition that they are descendants of Phut, one of the sons of Ham. Edmond D. Morel, in his book *Affairs of West Africa*, (published 1902), stated that the Fulani had a peculiar "knowledge of Jewish history." Quoting the French linguist De Guiraudon, the book goes on to state that the Fulani could not "have acquired their knowledge merely through Arabic sources…Moses and Abraham might have been individuals of the same race as themselves…it would seem as if the Puls (Fulani), if they themselves did not profess the Jewish faith…were at least in permanent contact with the Jewish people in remote times, and that, influenced at one time or another by the Israelites, they received Old Testament legends directly from them." We conclude with one last striking point by De Guiraudon about the Fulani: What they knew about Yeshua in the New Testament was very distorted, as if the message had reached them in a vague, fragmented condition.

Omar ibn Said acknowledged in his account that, "General Jim Owen and his wife used to read the gospel…they read it to me very much…For the law was given by Moses but grace and truth were by the Jesus *the Messiah*."

Question: Had Omar heard about Yeshua when he lived in West Africa – or had he learned this for the first time, that Yeshua was the Messiah? Another preserved account is that of Bilali Mohammed, an enslaved man on a plantation in Sapelo Island, Georgia during the American War of 1812. Bilali was Muslim, and could speak and write Arabic, but his first language was Fula. In another account, Salih Bilali – born around 1790 near the Niger River in Massina, Mali – his enslaver estimated that around a dozen people spoke Fula on his plantation at St. Simons Island, Georgia during 1812. It is very possible that these enslaved Fulani who were brought to America were formerly Jews, or possibly their ancestors were.

It is documented the persecution and pressure the Black Jews faced from Muslim tribes in Africa. For example, in 1492, when Askia Muhammed came to power in the region of Timbuktu, he decreed that Jews must convert to Islam or face expulsion. In 1526, the historian Leo Africanus wrote: "The king is a declared enemy of the Jews. He will not allow any to live in the city if he hears it said that a Berber merchant frequents them or does business with them he confiscates his goods." A nomad Jewish tribe called Daggatun, living in the Algerian Sahara as late as the 1850's, whose origins dated back to the 17th Century, had been pressured by the rulers of that region to convert to Islam, which they resisted. As a result, the Daggatun had been exiled to the desert. Gradually they lost their Jewish practices and eventually became Muslim. Similar accounts have been documented. One ethnologist in the 1920's said that he "was unable to distinguish a Jew from a Mohammedan while passing along the streets of Algiers, Constantine, and Tunis. It is remarkable that among the non-Jewish natives there are seen many Jews of Negroid type." So likewise, without a doubt, many of the enslaved who were brought to the American South were very likely Jews who had now begun to identify as Muslim.

There is something else further about the two enslaved men, London and Omar ibn Said. It is incredible how London was able to write English using Arabic characters to the Gullah dialect. William B. Hodgson, a world-leading philologist, and the person who received London's manuscript after his death, said this: "The manuscript of London is remarkable for precision in the use of the vowel points-harchat of the Arabic grammar…I infer from this, that as London was accustomed in making copies of the Koran with the same reverential sentiment he used the vowel points in copying the Bible of his adopted religion." Without doubt, both London and Omar ibn Said came from highly educated backgrounds. Both men could read and write Arabic. Did they both speak the same form of Arabic? Although the answer to that question is unknown, apparently there existed different forms of Arabic and dialects in the Middle Ages, and even in earlier times.

There was an eventual shift from predominant Hebrew-speaking to Arabic-speaking among Jews, as a result of the Muslim Conquest. Three forms of language that Jews spoke in early times, besides Hebrew, were Judaeo-Spanish, Judeo-Arabic, and Andalusi Arabic. By around 800 CE, most Jews within the Muslim Empire spoke Arabic. Judaeo-Spanish was spoken in Moorish Spain before and after the Alhambra Decree of Expulsion. It incorporated many Hebrew, Aramaic, and Arabic words, and was spoken also in North Africa and in the Levant. Judeo-Arabic dialects were spoken by Jewish communities in the Arab world, and came about due to Hebrew words, and migration. Andalusi Romance was the main language spoken in Iberia before the Moors came in 711. However, gradually it was replaced by Andalusi Arabic during the rule of the Berber-Moors and Arab-Muslims.

So again, why were so few accounts *found* of Black Jews in America? Because by the time millions of enslaved Jews had arrived, many of them were speaking Arabic, not Hebrew, and they no longer *identified* as being a Hebrew Jew. Why? *Because many no longer knew they were Hebrew Jews, even though they were.* Many had already begun identifying as Muslim due to assimilation. This also applies to Palestinians in the Gaza region today, as many of their ancestors were the original Jews even though the majority of Palestinians identify as Arab Muslim.

However today, with new technology available, many have been able to identify their ancestry and, in several cases, even identify their enslaved ancestors by means of modern genetic DNA testing. Also, we are able to understand a clearer picture of the history of human migrations due to DNA analysis and genetic sequencing. This is also being used to try and learn the origins of the early Jews in biblical times, and in answering the question of who were the original Jews.

One such effort in that endeavor were the results of a DNA project in 2011, entitled "The History of African Gene Flow into Southern European, Levantines, and Jews." (See Notes) From this testing, it was discovered that people from Southern Europe, Palestine, Israel, Syria, and Jordan have inherited genetic material of African origin. It was found that Syrian Jews, Iranian Jews, Iraqi Jews, Greek Jews, Turkish Jews, Italian Jews, and Ashkenazi Jews were detected with 3%-5% sub-Saharan African ancestry. These findings were explained as "evidence" regarding the "common origin" of those Jewish groups. The exact date of this African admixture was not determined, but it was estimated to have taken place between 1,600 and 3,400 years ago, or in other words, between the 15th Century BCE and the 5th Century CE. The researchers involved in that project went on to state that, although it was known the Mizrahi Iranian and Iraqi Jews had descended in part from the Jews who were exiled in Babylon in the 7th Century BCE, the researchers were amazed that they shared African admixture. The researchers concluded that the Jewish groups that participated descend from a "common ancestral population" which is "admixed with Africans," and "prior" to the Jewish Diaspora which occurred between the 8th and 6th Century BCE.

Another interesting example is the test analysis conducted in 2012 involving North African Jews, Ethiopian Jews, and Yemenite Jews. This testing presented the results that North African Jewish populations form distinct clusters with genetic proximity to each other and to "Middle Eastern (Palestine) groups." North African Jewish populations also showed proximity to European Jewish groups. For Ethiopian Jewish population groups, the results showed they were *most closely* related to *non-Jewish* Libyans and South Moroccans, and then to other North African and Middle Eastern *non-Jewish* populations. The real question that should be raised here is: Were the "non-Jewish" populations (that were so labeled) have at one time been "Jewish?" Who – or what – gets to determine what is labeled *Jewish* verses *non-Jewish*? What if a certain segment of a population is historically viewed as Jewish, whereas another segment of the population is historically *Not* considered Jewish? So there is a caution in demographic labeling in the gene pool of DNA testing analysis. (And finally, results of Yemenite Jewish populations in this particular analysis showed they were genetically closest to "Egyptians" followed by Middle Eastern "non-Jews." So here we go again. And, the findings did not specify if the "Egyptians" cited in the project were Jewish or non-Jewish).

One bright side is that the technology is constantly improving. Case in point is the sequencing of Mummy DNA. Years ago it was considered impossible. Now, the successful genomic testing on ancient Egyptian mummies is happening. Recently, the DNA of a vizier to King Tuthmosis III of the 15th Century BCE, was sequenced, whose name was Rekhmire. The testing results revealed that Rekhmire was Nubian.

All this to say is that we are reminded again, DNA testing analysis can in many ways help to tell the story of the history of human migration and of the Black Jews. But in other cases, the results may be flawed. One can never ignore or exclude the true history contained in the word of the Most High over modern-day technology, but is useful only when it is in complete harmony with Yehovah, the Great Historian, and his accurate chronology. His holy calendar of prophetic events includes the "Times of the Gentiles." The descendants of enslaved ancestors are looking for the answers as to where they are in the stream of time. They are searching as to *who they are.*

> *Will these descendants of their great-grandparents one day experience an awakening? Zephaniah 3:10 prophesied:*
>
> *"From the region of the rivers of Ethiopia the one entreating me, the daughter of my scattered ones will bring a gift to me."*

What if those scattered from the region of the rivers of Ethiopia are scattered *further beyond* – as a result of being transported by means of slave ships? Would they not still be considered as the scattered ones? Absolutely. Everyone must be located and found, no matter where they are scattered.

> *Will the Most High allow time for them to learn about the Seed of Judah during the Messiah's Second coming? When would the Second Coming be?*

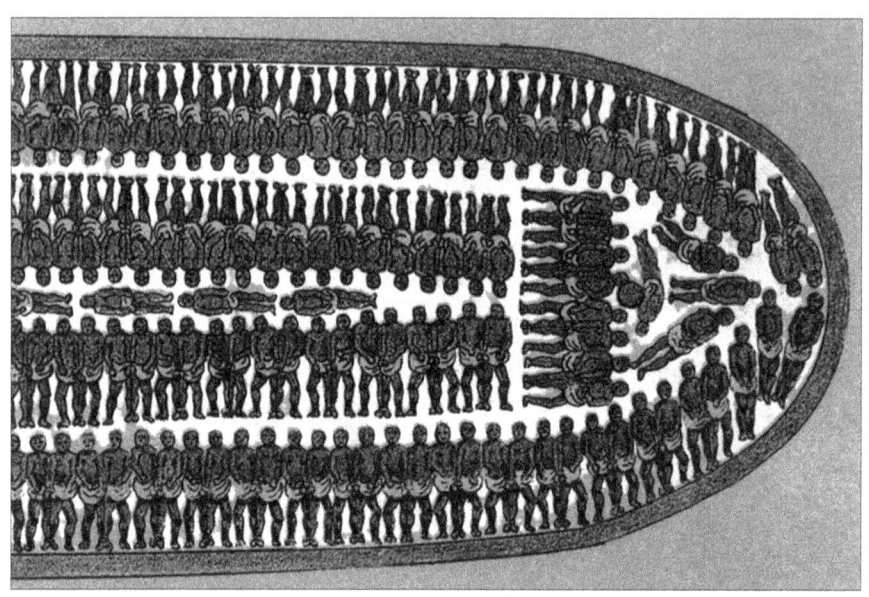

Middle Passage. Millions of enslaved persons, including black Jews, were brought to the Americas.

Slaves from Angola newspaper notice. The region around Angola was called "Land of the Jews."

Photos | 165

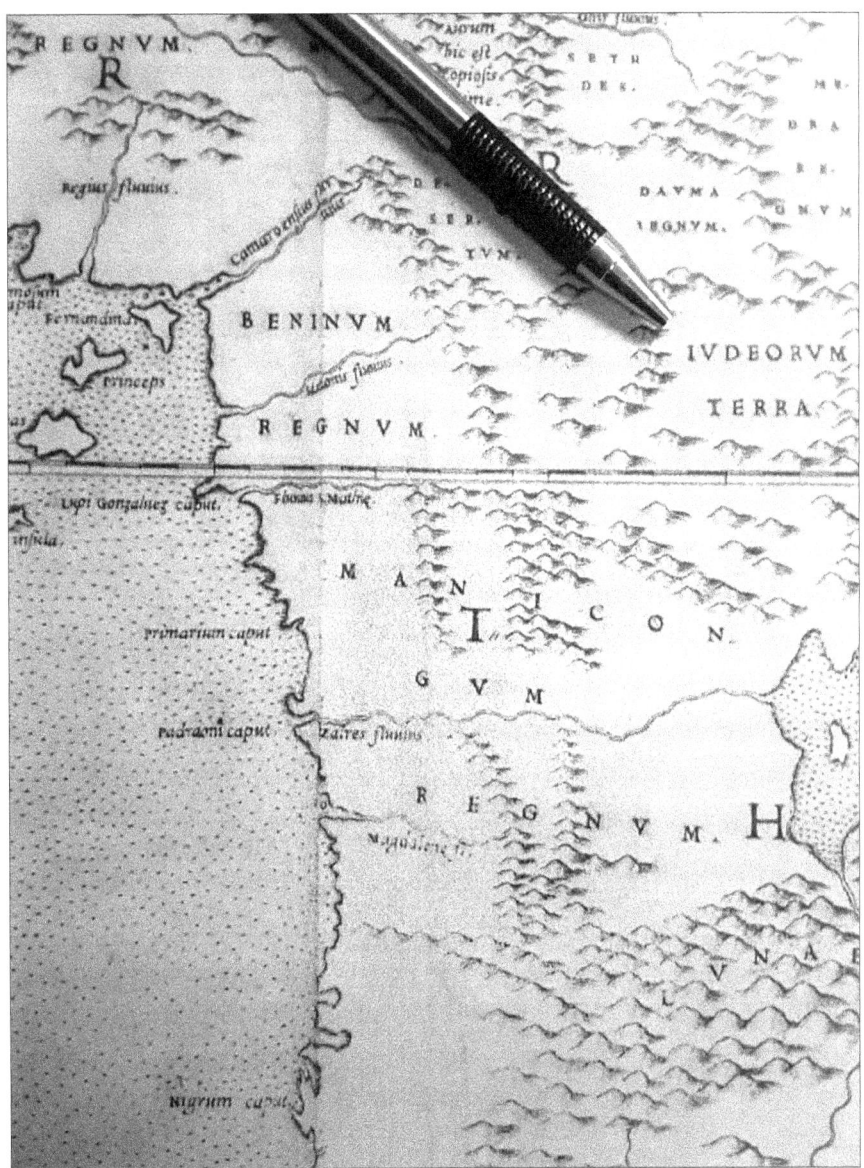

African Map of West/Central Africa, published in 1588.

Resized Map closeup of the Congo, IVDEORVM TERRA, the "Land of the Jews."

Photos | 167

(Resized) Map of Kingdom of Juda" (Whydah/Ouidah) in 1747, located in Dahomey/Benin, West Africa. Millions were shipped from this port.

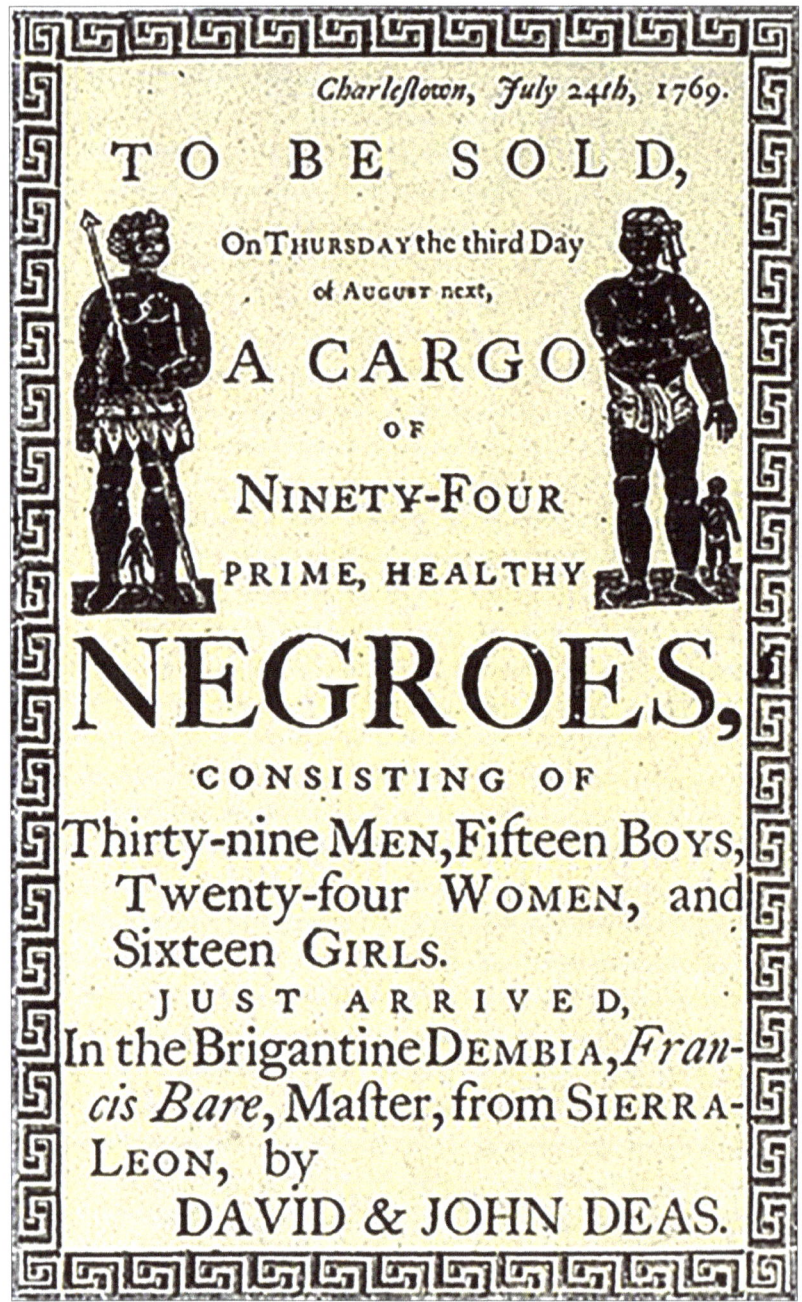

Newspaper Auction of NEGROES for sale. The word "Negro" was a Portuguese and Spanish word for "Black."

Photos | 169

The slave ship Clotilda which landed in Mobile, Alabama, 1860.
The ship left the West Coast slave port of Ouidah (Juda) carrying enslaved from Dahomey/Benin.

Map of Central America and Caribbean.

Gaza City, Palestine. Some from the Tribe of Ephraim settled here. Descendants from Ephraim may still be there today.

Photos | 171

World War One. 1914-1918. Times of the Gentiles ended.

Tunis, Tunisia in 1899. Many Jews lived there.

CHAPTER 15

The Coronation of Messiah the Seed of Judah

As was said at the beginning of this discussion in Chapter One, there are two groups of people – those of every tribe and people, and those from the original people – who must be given an opportunity to understand that prophecy in Eden about the Coming Seed who would crush the head of the Serpent, the one given the name Satan and devil, names that were given to him because of his course of action of becoming a resister and slanderer of the Most High and His will & purpose. So let an examination begin about that Messianic Seed's second appearance.

Just as the prophet Daniel, in the book that bears his name, spoke of the Messiah's first Coming in the year 29 CE in the prophecy of the 70 weeks, let us read Daniel Chapter 4, which gives us the year for the Messiah's second appearance and presence (Dan 4,5,10-17,24,25,36):

> "I, Nebuchadnezzar…there was a dream that I beheld, and it began to make me afraid…In the visions of my head while on my bed, I saw a tree in the midst of the earth, and its height was enormous. The tree grew and became strong, and its top reached the heavens, and it was visible to the ends of the whole earth. Its foliage was beautiful, and its frit was

abundant, and there was food on it for all. Beneath it the beasts of the field would seek shade, and on its branches, the birds of the heavens would dwell, and all creatures would feed from it. As I viewed the visions of my head while on my bed, I saw a watcher, a holy one, coming down from the heavens. He called out loudly: "Chop down the tree, cut off its branches, shake off its leaves, and scatter its fruit! Let the beasts flee from beneath it, and the birds from its branches. But leave the stump with its roots in the ground, with a banding of iron and of copper, among the grass of the field. Let it be wet with the dew of the heavens, and let its portion be with the beasts among the vegetation of the earth. Let its heart be changed from that of a human, and let it be given the heart of a beast, *and let seven times pass over it.*"

"This is by the decree or watchers, and the request is by the word of the holy ones, so that people living may know that the Most High is Ruler in the kingdom of mankind and that he gives it to whomever he wants, and he sets up over it even the lowliest of men."

"This is the interpretation, O king…and you they will be driving away from men, and with the beasts of the field your dwelling will come to be…and seven times themselves will pass over you until you know that the Most High is Ruler in the kingdom of mankind, and that to the one whom he wants to he gives it."

As we read, King Nebuchadnezzar of ancient Babylon, who had taken the entire Kingdom of Judah as prisoners, had a dream of an enormous tree. The tree was chopped down and the king lost his sanity, but after 7 years he regains his sanity and his rulership is restored. However, we must remember that this prophecy was not all about Nebuchadnezzar. He had taken the Most High's people captive. More importantly, Nebuchadnezzar had removed the Judean king from off the throne of Judah. So this dream was not only about when Nebuchadnezzar would regain his rulership. That was only an initial fulfillment of the prophecy. The real meaning of the dream had to do with when the kingdom of Judah would be restored.

In the major meaning of this dream, the symbolic tree represented the Israelite kings who represented the Most High's rulership and sovereignty here on earth. When was that tree in the dream chopped down? It was in 607 BCE, when Nebuchadnezzar's Babylonian armies destroyed Jerusalem, interrupting the line of Israelite kings. When would the Israelite kingship be restored? Would that also be in 7 years just like it was for Nebuchadnezzar? No, the Israelite kingship was not restored 7 years after 607 BCE. In fact, there never was another genealogical heir since 607 BCE who had been anointed as king and sat on the throne to restore the Judean kingship on earth during the prophetic time period. How? Because this time period became known as the *Gentile Times*, when Jerusalem would be trampled by the nations while no royal heir would ascend the throne to represent Yehovah's sovereignty on earth. So this fact reveals that the 7 times has a greater meaning than 7 literal years. These are 7 *prophetic years*.

How long would the 7 prophetic years be? The scriptural pattern, or rule, is "a day for a year, a day for a year" (Numbers 14:34; Ezekiel 7:3). Unlike the prophecy of the "Seventy weeks," this prophetic dream has no mention of weeks, only of years. So by calculating the length of the 7 times using the prophetic code of "a day for a year," we are presented with the mathematical calculus of 360 times 7, since the Hebrew Jews counted in months of thirty days each. We can establish this by noting in the Book of Genesis that time was divided into months of thirty days (Genesis 7:11,24; Genesis 8:3,4; Revelation 12:6,14). At Deuteronomy 34:8, it says when Moses died, the sons of Israel wept for thirty days. Even the Egyptians developed a calendar of lunar months of thirty days each. So, by calculating 360 days in a biblical year times 7, the sum of the equation is 2520 days, and then by converting the days into years, we arrive at 2520 *years* as the accurate length of the prophetic *seven times* in Nebuchadnezzar's dream.

The Israelite kingship was interrupted when Nebuchadnezzar captured King Zedekiah and tried to replace him with governor Gedaliah in the seventh month of Tishri 607 BCE (2 Kings 25:6,7,22,25). The 2520 years would begin counting then. Even Yeshua recognized when he was still living on earth that the Gentile Times would extend into the future beyond his day when he said:

> "However, when you see Jerusalem surrounded by encamped armies, then know that the desolating of her has drawn hear…and they will fall by the edge of the sword and be led captive into all the nations, ***and Jerusalem will be trampled on by the nations until the appointed times of the Gentiles are fulfilled.*** " (Luke 21:24)

There is no questionable doubt at all to the year 607 BCE as being when the 7 prophetic years began counting. Several historical sources also establish that 537 BCE was when the Hebrew Jews returned to Judah, in fulfillment of another prophecy that the Jews would be in captivity for seventy years, as stated in the Book of Ezra. The Encyclopedia Americana states that the Book of Ezra covers the history of the returning exiles "from 537 BC." If one counts back 70 years from 537 BCE, they will arrive at 607 BCE, the year the Jews were taken from Judah and brought to Babylon. Additionally, even in 537 BCE, when the Jews returned to Judah, the Most High Yehovah's sovereignty, as symbolized by the throne of Judah, still had not been restored. This was because Zerubbabel was not anointed and made *king* when he returned to Jerusalem. He was only appointed as a *governor* of Judah (Haggai 1:1; 2:21).

So just as Daniel's prophecy about the "Seventy Weeks" foretold when the Messiah would first appear, this prophecy about the *seven times* is foretelling when the Messiah would return, his second Coming. Since the *seven times* is understood to mean a time period of 2,520 years (the Times of the Gentiles), we can logically discern that the Gentile Times would extend into the time period called "the Last Days" of the world. There is a connection between the Gentile Times and the Last Days. This is shown to be the case by looking at what else Yeshua said to his disciples that same hour he spoke to them about the Gentile Times. Yeshua was asked by his disciples, "Master, but when shall these things be? and what sign will there be when these things shall come to pass?" The disciples' question had been prompted because of what Yeshua had stated to them moments earlier about the temple in Jerusalem. Yeshua revealed to them that the temple would be destroyed:

> "And as some spake of the temple, how it was adorned with goodly stones and gifts, he said, As for these things which ye behold, the days will come, in the which there shall not be left one stone upon another, that shall not be thrown down… Nation shall rise against nation, and kingdom against kingdom, and great earthquakes shall be in divers places, and famines, and pestilences…But before all these, they shall lay their hands on you, and persecute you, delivering you up to

the synagogues, and into prisons, and ye shall be betrayed both by parents, and brethren, and kinsfolks, and friends; and some of you shall they cause to be put to death." (Luke 21:5,6,10-12,16)

The followers of Yeshua would be put to death. However, although the persecution and martyrdom would come about at the hands of political kings, soldiers, courts, even by friends and family members – who would be the *instigators* behind those attacks on the original Hebrew and Greek-speaking Christians? One of them would be the "Man of Lawlessness" that was touched upon in Chapter Twelve. The Apostles Paul and Peter both wrote about this coming Apostasy, and Yeshua warned about it in his parable of the Wheat and Weeds.

This "Man of Lawlessness" is not an individual, but is a collective group, a revolt, a planned deliberate rebellion and apostasy. They are part of the serpent's seed. The Benjamite Paul foretold, "Let no one seduce you in any manner, because it will not come unless the apostasy comes first and the man of lawlessness gets revealed, the son of destruction, and lifts himself up over everyone who is called god or an object of reverence, so that he sits down in the temple of The God, publicly showing himself to be a god…but the lawless one's presence is according to the operation of Satan with every powerful work and lying signs and portents…" (2 Thessalonians 2:3,4,9)

The Apostle Peter also alerted the original Hebrew and Greek-speaking Christians, "There will also be false teachers among you. These very ones will quietly bring in destructive sects and will disown even the owner that bought them, bringing speedy destruction upon themselves."

(2 Peter 2:1) Yeshua warned his followers of this coming defection in his parable about the Wheat and the Weeds when he said:

> The kingdom of the heavens has become like a man that sowed fine seed in his field. While men were sleeping, his enemy came and oversowed weeds in among the wheat…the slaves of the householder came up and said to him, Master, did you not sow fine seed in your field? How, then, does it come to have weeds? He said to them, an enemy, a man did this. They said to him, Do you want us, then, to go out and collect them? He said, No…**let both grow together until the harvest**, and in the harvest season I will tell the reapers, First collect the weeds and bind them in bundles to burn them up, then go to gathering the wheat into my storehouse." (Matthew 13:25-30)

The other instigator who would incite persecutions and deaths upon the followers of Yeshua, and twist the truth of his teachings, is the one mentioned in Revelation as "Babylon the Great":

> "So he carried me away in the spirit of the wilderness: And I saw a woman sit upon a scarlet colored beast, full of names of blasphemy, having seven heads and ten horns. And the woman was arrayed in purple and scarlet colour, and decked with gold and precious stones and pearls, having a golden cup in her hand full of abominations and filthiness of her fornication, and upon her forehead was a name written, MYSTERY, BABYLON THE GREAT, THE MOTHER OF HARLOTS AND ABOMINATIONS OF THE EARTH." (Revelation 17: 3-5)

Notice that Babylon the Great is a symbolic woman, a harlot or prostitute, who commits sexual fornication with "the Kings of the earth." Notice also that the symbolic woman Babylon the Great is riding a wild beast. This beast symbolizes all the kings of the earth, all the political systems of the earth, which do the bidding of the prostitute. This harlot is called Babylon the Great because she promotes and teaches false religious worship, all the false religious pagan customs and teachings that began in ancient Babylon Chaldea – the teachings of demons – such as hellfire, triune gods and goddesses, spiritism, talking to the dead, the crucifix, a clergy priesthood, and much more demon-inspired teachings.

If the grotesque scene of a prostitute riding a seven-headed wild beast with ten horns was not shocking enough, then notice the next scene presented in the revelation regarding this unclean harlot:

> "And I saw that the woman was drunk with the blood of the holy ones and with the blood of the witnesses of Yeshua." (Revelation 17:6)

This false religious world-wide system, Babylon the Great, has instigated and provoked a gross amount of religious and political hatred on the Hebrew and Greek-speaking followers of Yeshua. Note a few historical sources that show how the original Hebrew Christians were treated during the Roman Empire while under the influence and control of the harlot:

A great fire erupted in Rome in 64 CE, destroying one fourth of the city. According to historian Tacitus, it was rumored that Emperor Nero was responsible, and to protect himself blamed the original Christians. This resulted in mass arrests of Yeshua's followers, who were tortured, many put to death, and some burned alive.

Christians refused sacrifice to the emperor, and very few of the Christians recanted. All a prisoner had to do was scatter a pinch of incense on the flame and he would be given a Certificate of Sacrifice and turned free. It was also carefully explained to him that he was not worshipping the emperor; merely acknowledging the divine character of the emperor as head of the Roman state. Still, almost no Christians availed themselves of the chance to escape.

The first Christians thought it was wrong to fight, and would not serve in the army even when the Empire needed soldiers.

Christians refused to enter the army or to take any part in war. Origen remarked that Christians could not engage in war against any nation. They have learned from their leader that they are children of peace. In that period many Christians were martyred for refusing military service.

The early Christians were arrested and flogged for preaching from house to house, as Yeshua had trained them to do.

The Benjamite Hebrew Paul was put to death during the rule of Nero, sometime between 65-68 CE

Even hatred against the Bible itself and anyone questioning the pope was displayed by Babylon the Great in the Middle Ages:

John Wycliff, a Bible translator, questioned the Papacy. Wycliff believed in translating the Bible into the common Vernacular so people could read and study it. After Wycliff's death in 1384, Pope Martin V confirmed that his corpse be exhumed and his bones to be burned. His ashes were done away with in the River Swift in 1428, forty-four years after Wycliff's death.

William Tyndale, a translator of the Bible into English, which infuriated the Papacy, whose policy was against the common people reading or possessing a Bible. Tyndale was arrested, and in 1536 was convicted of heresy, executed by strangulation, and then burnt at the stake.

Michael Servetus, a Spanish theologian and physician. He rejected the Trinity and other unscriptural doctrines and was condemned by the Papacy. Servetus was burned at the stake in 1553.

Just as Yeshua had said in answer to the question his disciples had asked about the sign of his second return or presence, persecution of his followers would continue in the last days. In his parable of the wheat and weeds, Yeshua said that both will grow together until the "harvest", which Yeshua said meant "is a conclusion of a system of things" (or End of the world; End of the age, Matthew 13:39).

So the Gentile Times has a direct connection and bearing on the time period referred to as the "End of the world." In fact, the Gentile Times has a direct connection to the Book of Revelation, since that book covers the events of the "Last Days" in symbolic language. What was the whole point of Nebuchadnezzar's dream? It was that after 7 times had passed, the royal kingship of Judah would be restored, and, as the dream indicated, "so that people living may know he gives it (the Kingdom) to whomever he wants." Notice the Most High's choice in who would restore the royal kingship in Revelation, Chapters 11 & 12. When the seventh angel blew his trumpet, Revelation 11:15 says:

> "And the seventh angel blew his trumpet. And loud voices occurred in heaven, saying: The Kingdom of the world did become the Kingdom of our Lord and of his Christ (Messiah), and he will rule as king forever and ever."

This text is referring to the coronation of Hamashiach!

The vision tells us that the royal kingship is finally restored at the end of the Gentile Times.

How long is the Gentile Times, and when would it end? We have already established that Nebuchadnezzar's dream of "7 times" is a prophetic time period of 2,520 years, counting from 607 BCE when the Hebrew Jews of Judah were taken captive to Babylon and the royal kingship of Judah was temporarily cutoff until the 2,520 years end. When would that be? From 607 BCE, 2,520 years would end in 1914 CE.

Is there evidence that the true Mashiach returned in the year 1914 and restored the royal kingship as the Coming Seed foretold in Eden? Yes, there is.

Is there evidence of an "Awakening" and a "Re-gathering" taking place right now of dispersed people during the royal reign of the true Messiah? Yes, there is.

Let's first look at the evidence that Mashiach did return in 1914, and who was he:

- In the vision of the 4 horsemen of the Apocalypse in Revelation chapter six, the rider of the white horse was given "a crown." (Rev. 6:2)

- The rider of the red horse "took peace away from the earth, so that they would slaughter one another; and a "great sword" was given him." (Rev. 6:4)

- Yeshua said that at the time of his second return, "Nation shall rise against Nation, and Kingdom against Kingdom." (Matt. 24:6)

- When the seventh angel blew his trumpet, loud voices in heaven announced "the Kingdom of the world did become the Kingdom of our Lord and of his Christ (Messiah), and he will rule forever and ever." (Rev. 11:15)

- After loud voices in heaven announced the Kingdom of the Lord's Messiah (Christ), a war broke out in heaven and the one called Devil and Satan and his angels were thrown down to the earth. (Rev. 12:7-12)

- In Sept/Oct 1914 (the Hebrew month of Tishri), World War I began. At that time, historians called it the "Great War" because no war of that kind had ever occurred before in terms of its size and modern weaponry.

- The final overthrow of Judah by Nebuchadnezzar occurred in the month of Tishri, 607 BCE

- The Messiah's Return would be an invisible presence, based on Matthew 24:3, where it says the "Sign of your *Parousia*" in the Greek translation. The Greek word *Parousia* means "Presence", as having come, arrived; Not "Coming", as "on the way." If someone is *physically* present, there is no need for a "Sign."

Conclusion: Yeshua is the true Messiah. He was the Coming Seed as prophesied in Eden. Yeshua is a direct descendant of Judah, and restored the royal kingship. He has been ruling invisibly from his throne in Heaven since 1914 to gather together a dispersed people in these Last Days.

One final point regarding 1914:

There was a millennial Bible study group in the late 19th century called the "International Bible Students Association, who were based in America. This Bible group had rejected all of the mainstream "Christian" religions because they felt those religions were promoting pagan babylonish beliefs in their church doctrines, such as hellfire, the Trinity, Immortality of the Soul, and other teachings. The International Bible Students felt it was important that they root out any such pagan customs as soon as it was discerned from the Bible, and dedicate themselves to returning to the original teachings of Jesus. They also were very committed to understanding Bible prophecy, especially in relation to the Lord's Second Coming.

When studying Daniel's prophecy about Nebuchadnezzar's dream, the Bible Students understood that the Gentile Times was 2,520 years long. They published this understanding in their publications which were distributed worldwide in several languages, and would often incorporate such statements as 'The times of the Gentiles would expire with the year 1914' and 'the Times of the Gentiles will run fully out with the year A.D. 1914, when Christ's Kingdom would be established' (publications in 1876, 1881, 1891, & 1904). The Bible Students also believed that Jesus' return would remain invisible, not in a fleshly body. In 1933, this study group changed their name to "Jehovah's Witnesses." (See Notes)

Is there an "Awakening" and a "Re-gathering" taking place right now of dispersed persons during the royal reign of Yeshua Hamashiach? Yes! Consider the following news developments in these Last Days:

> One of the ethnic groups in Nigeria are the Igbo. Among this group are the Igbo Jews, who say their ancestors were Jews. According to them, they are descendants of Eri, the son of Gad, who was one of the twelve sons of Jacob.

In eastern Senegal near the border of Mali is a settlement of 4,000 people called Bani Israel. Even though they are Muslim, they say they are descended from Egyptian Jews who left Egypt to Somalia, and then to Nigeria, where they split about 1,000 years ago. One branch of the family went to Mali, while the other went to Guinea.

In Benin there is a large Jewish community. They have the Hebrew Pentateuch. This African Jewish group were discovered in the 1920's.

In Ghana there are the Jews in the town of Sefwi Wiawso, who, according to their oral history, lived in Mali until 400 years ago when they were persecuted and moved to Ivory Coast where they stayed for 250 years until they were persecuted again and moved to Ghana, where they have been for the last 150 years.

Near Timbuktu, Mali there is a group of 1,000 crypto-Jews who practice Judaism secretly for fear of persecution.

In the Sahara are Yoruba Jews. They say their ancestors were driven from place to place by Moslem persecution until they reached Mali. These descendants were discovered in the 1920's, when there were about 2,000 people in twenty villages and they called themselves B'nai Ephraim. One of the tribes of the Northern Israelite kingdom was the part Hamitic tribe of Ephraim. Yeroboam I was the first king of the Northern kingdom. Sadly, the Northern kingdom plunged into idolatry and formed an apostate religion. But some Ephraimites returned to the Kingdom of Judah. Today, some believe about the Yoruba Jews that the name "Yoruba" came from the name "Yeroboam" the first king of the ten-tribes.

In Zimbabwe are the Lemba Jews, whose ancestors left Judea about 2,500 years ago and settled in Yemen, and later in Ethiopia. At some point the tribe split. Some stayed in Ethiopia while others migrated further to Southeastern Africa.

In Cote d'Ivoire are large groups of indigenous people called the Danites, who say they descend from the Israelite tribe of Dan.

There were 400,000 Israelites discovered in Cameroon in 1920.

Descendants from the tribes of Ephraim and Manasseh lived in the territories of Palestine (at time of printing, Palestinian territory is under heavy bombardment from Israeli forces. Reports of close to 17,000 Palestinian deaths).

Many of the Palestinians are descendants of the original Jews.

Recent DNA genetic analysis show North African and Sub-Saharan African ancestry detected among Jewish populations in the Levant.

In other places all over the world, people are hearing for the first time about Black Jews. Many people are learning & investigating their ancestry, including Jewish roots. Why is this happening now? Notice what Isaiah and Yeshua said:

"And it must occur in that day that Jehovah will again offer his hand a second time, to acquire the remnant of his people who will remain over from Assyria and from Egypt and from Pathros and from Cush and from Elam and from Shinar and from Hamath and from the islands of the sea. And he will certainly rise up a signal for the nations and gather the dispersed ones of Israel; and the scattered ones of Judah he will collect together from the four extremities of the earth." (Isaiah 11:11,12)

"…go continually to the lost sheep of the house of Israel… And I have other sheep, which are not of this fold; those also I must bring…" (Matthew 10:6; John 10:16)

We notice in Isaiah that Yehovah said He will offer his hand again *a second time* to gather the scattered ones of Judah. And Yeshua stated to "*Go continually* to the lost sheep of the house of Israel.

Not only were the Most High's people scattered as a result of the deportation in 732 BCE and that of Babylon in 607 BCE, but also the dispersion that resulted from the destruction of Jerusalem by the Romans in 70 CE. Even Yeshua's Hebrew followers were scattered, fleeing to the mountains of Pella and other regions. What later happened to Yeshua's followers years after the destruction of Jerusalem and its temple? Part of that answer is derived from the visions in Revelation. Towards the end of the 1st Century CE, the Revelation revealed there were seven congregations in the Roman province of Asia, which later became part of the country of Turkey. So Yeshua's Hebrew followers, along with gentile converts, helped spearhead Yeshua's teachings into the region of Turkey, as well as into Africa. The seven congregations were Ephesus, Smyrna, Pergamum, Thyatira, Sardis, Philadelphia, Laodicea.

These congregations experienced much opposition and persecution from their enemies. For example, Yeshua sent this message from heaven to the congregation in Smyrna:

> "I know thy works and tribulation and poverty (but thou art rich) and I know the blasphemy of them which say they are Jews, and are not, but are the synagogue of Satan. Fear none of those things which thou shalt suffer: Behold, the devil shall cast some of you into prison that ye may be tried; and ye shall have tribulation ten days: Be thou faithful unto death, and I will give thee a crown of life." (Rev. 2:9,10)

About 59 years after Yeshua sent that message, an 86 year old man named Polycarp was burned and stabbed to death at the city of Smyrna for being a follower of Yeshua. According to The Martyrdom of Polycarp, when wood was being gathered for the execution, the Jews were extremely zealous in assisting at this, even though it would take place on a great Sabbath day. Another congregation that faced persecution was the one in Philadelphia. Yet note the outcome:

> "Look! I will give those from the synagogue of Satan who say they are Jews, and yet they are not but are lying – look! I will make them come and do obeisance before your feet and make them know I have loved you." (Rev. 3:9)

Yes, the persecution from the local enemies was great, however, notice the outcome – these misguided Jews, who hated their Hebrew brothers for following Yeshua – some of those haters ended up following Yeshua too!

Edom was the name of Esau, Jacob's twin brother. Even though the Edomites, the descendants of Edom, no longer existed as a people after the destruction of Jerusalem, the name *Edom* in future prophetic scripture would continue to symbolize *the enemies of the Most High's people, regardless of race*, whom the Most High has denounced forever. (Malachi 1:1-4; Obadiah 10,18)

We are living at a time than no other before now. The Most High is giving those whose ancestors were once in a covenant relationship with Him one more opportunity to come back and become part of the new arrangement He has setup in these last days. The Most High is a loving God. He does not want anyone to lose *life*.

So what do we need to do to be saved?

(See Notes)

CHAPTER 16

What Do We Need to Do to Be Saved?

"Out of Egypt I Called My Son" (Matthew 2:15)

We are living in exciting times right now. The Most High said through his prophet Ezekiel that He would re-gather the dispersed ones back:

> "For this is what the Sovereign Lord Jehovah has said: "Here I am, I myself, and I will search for my sheep and care for them…The lost one I shall search for, and the dispersed one I shall bring back, and the broken one I shall bandage and the ailing one I shall strengthen…" (Ezekiel 34:11,16)

Yeshua, when on earth, carried out his assignment and instructions that his father the Most High had given him regarding the lost sheep. We recall when Yeshua entered the region of Tyre and Sidon and encountered a woman who was not a Jew:

> "And, look! A Canaanite woman from those regions came out and cried aloud, saying: "Have mercy on me, Lord, Son of David. My daughter is badly demonized…In answer he said: I was not sent forth to any but to the lost sheep of the house of Israel." (Matthew 15:22-24)

Yeshua's assignment while on earth was to minister to the lost sheep of the house of Israel. It was not yet time to minister and baptize people of the nations, the Gentiles. That assignment would come later. According to Daniel's prophecy of the Seventy Weeks, it would be at the end of the "one week" when the Law Covenant would end, and then a new assignment would begin – making disciples from people of all the nations, and being a Jewish proselyte would no longer be a requirement to be baptized (Daniel 9:27). Such was the case with the Italian Cornelius who was not an Israelite or proselyte. Daniel 9:27 says:

> "And he shall confirm the covenant with many for **one week**: and in the middle of the week he shall cause the sacrifice and gift offering to cease"

Yeshua was put to death in 33 CE, in the middle of the "one week," which began in 29 CE when Yeshua was baptized and became the Messiah. The end of the "one week" would be 36 CE, and the completion of the "Seventy years" prophecy. The blessings of the covenant that the Most High made with Abraham would be extended to Abraham's Hebrew offspring. But at the end of the "one week" Yehovah's covenant with Abraham would extend an invitation to the nations. When the invisible Yeshua told Peter, "Stop calling defiled the things God has cleansed," Peter responded, God is not partial, but in every nation the man who fears him and does what is right is acceptable to him(Acts 10:15-48).

But that new arrangement had not come yet. However, the Canaanite-Phoenician woman was persistent. The account continues:

> "When the woman came she began doing obeisance to him, saying: Lord, help me! In answer he said: it is not right to

take the bread of the children and throw it to *little dogs (kunarion)*." She said, Yes, Lord, but really the *little dogs (kunarion)* do eat of the crumbs falling from the table of their masters." (Matthew 15:25-27)

According to the Law, dogs were unclean animals. The term was used as a derogatory metaphor on Gentiles as to say they were morally unclean. The Greek word for "dog" was *Kuon*, such as a "wild dog." But Yeshua used a diminutive, when translated into Greek is *Kunarion*, meaning "little dog, a puppy." In texts of the Greek Scriptures, diminutives are often used to indicate affection and familiarity, such as "little sheep", or "little children." So by likening the woman to a "little dog" or puppy, and the Hebrew Israelites to "children", Yeshua was indicating who would be spiritually fed first according to his assignment.

However, notice what happened:

"Then Yeshua answered and said unto her, O woman, great is thy faith; be it unto thee even as thou wish. And her daughter was made whole from that very hour."

Here is the beauty of the Most High Jah! The Most High without a doubt gave Yeshua the wisdom and discernment to administer *mercy* whenever the circumstances allowed it. The Most High has full confidence in His son, and trusts that whatever actions he takes will never be outside the boundaries of his assigned role. Praise Jah, that He is not rigid when it comes to mercy, just as David and Bathsheba learned, who, according to the Law, should have received the death penalty because of their sin.

We are witnessing events right now in our lifetime that the prophets spoke about. People are being awakened and gathered as never before, so that they can be reconnected to the promises that their ancestors had lost contact with thousands of years ago. The Transatlantic Slave Trade and the Arab Slave Trade severed millions, billions, from the prophecies of the foretold Seed of Judah that was to come. Many Jews came as slaves to America, but did not know their past. Many Jews came as Muslims, because they had assimilated while in Africa. But now we are seeing many African-Americans, some "direct descendants" of their Israelite ancestors, who are processing this lost history. And many in the Diaspora are doing the same.

Earlier we addressed DNA testing analysis. Keep in mind that genetic testing designed for those considered to have "Jewish Ancestry" is based primarily for groups who are not descendants of Shem, but of Ashkenaz. And we are glad they are learning of their ancestry too. This is only being pointed out so that those who are new to genealogy may be made aware of certain DNA testing for "Jewish ancestry" may exclude your haplotype. Those of you who *know* your history, may you never get downhearted. Be proud of your history, but not haughty. Be humbled of your history, but not humiliated. Just as the Most High has said, "Hear, you people, and give ear. Do not be haughty." And again He says, "O may the crushed one not return humiliated." And again the Most High says, "For Yehovah is high, and yet the humble one he sees."

We are witnessing prophecy. This is the greatest opportunity for all to learn the truth about the Most High, whose name is found in the Tetragrammaton, Yehovah (Igbo – Jehova; Yoruba – Jehofah; Samoan – Ieova; Cantonese –Yehwowah; Japanese – Ehoba; Vietnamese – Giehova; Somali – Yehowah), and of His Messiah.

Very soon, Babylon the Great, including apostate Christendom, will face her fast-approaching judgment and be done away with. The word Christendom is not referring to only one major church denomination. It is referring to all churches who "claim to be Christian" but their teachings and beliefs are promoting false pagan beliefs from ancient Babylon. No more provoking of ethnic and religious hatred and inciting of genocides. Revelation 17:16,17 tells us what is in store for her:

> "And the ten horns that you saw, and the wild beast, these will hate the harlot and will make her devastated and naked, and will eat up her fleshy parts and will completely burn her with fire. For God put it into their hearts to carry out his thought…until the words of God will have been accomplished."

Before the political kings of the world turn against this blood-guilty, hypocritical worldwide religious system, what is the first wisest thing we must do without delay? Notice what the Most High's servant John heard from above:

> "GET OUT OF HER, my people, if you do not want to share with her in her sins, and if you do not want to receive part of her plagues." (Revelation 18:4)

We cannot procrastinate. If we recognize that we are still supporting any type of faith or religion that does not recognize or follow the true Messiah Yeshua, or still observing celebrations that come from babylonish, pagan customs, or traditions and festivals of Law under the old arrangement, then we need to "Get Out of Her" without delay. Yeshua did not come to destroy the Law, but to fulfill it. The prophecy in Daniel said that the Messiah would "cause sacrifice and gift offering to cease." (Daniel 9:27) The only way for us to fulfill the Law is to follow the life pattern and teachings of our Messiah King under a new arrangement. He is our perfect exemplar.

When the cry "Peace and Security!" is heard, then sudden destruction will be instantly upon her, "as pangs of distress upon a pregnant woman, and they will by no means escape." Yeshua called this horrific event the "Great Tribulation." This world event will be sudden, unexpected. We must take action *Before* these events occur. (1 Thessalonians 5:3; Matthew 24:21)

Then, after the entire false religious system is destroyed, the kingdoms of the world will then attempt to eliminate the Most High's people at Har-Magedon, or the "Mountain of Megiddo" (Revelation 16:13,14,16). Megiddo was an ancient fortress city where many decisive battles were fought in biblical times. However, the "Mountain of Megiddo" that the "kings of the entire inhabited earth" gather for the final war will not be a literal location in the Levant or any other place. Revelation 16:16 says "And they gathered them together to the *place* that is called in Hebrew Har-Magedon." Notice the text said they are being gathered together to the "place." That word has more than one meaning. According to Vine's Expository Dictionary of New Testament words, the Greek word here is *topon*, which means 'a condition or situation.' The war of Har-Magedon, or Armadeddon, represents a *world situation*, in which all the kings and their armies are maneuvered by Satan and the demons into fighting against the Most High's people worldwide. But His servants will not raise a finger in this decisive war. He has delegated the battle to his Heavenly son Yeshua the King, and his Heavenly armies of mighty angels. This will be a time of great testing and faith in following the instructions for survival that will be made available only within the Most High's organizational arrangement that His people will be inside of.

It will be just like the days of Noah. Back during that critical time period, there was only ONE WAY of survival – getting inside the ark that Noah and his family had built. Everyone living at that time had the opportunity to discern the expressed will and purpose of the Most High God and to follow the new arrangement for survival that was open for them to be a part of. If anyone thought they were going to survive by creating their own arrangement – such as building their own boat or ship – they were gravely mistaken.

The same is very true today – there is only one way to survival – discerning the expressed will and purpose of the Most High God and to follow the arrangement that is being made available to us in these last days. The Benjamite Saul – he knew the Law forwards and backwards. Saul was well versed in the Hebrew Scriptures. And yet, he was hunting down and murdering the followers of Yeshua, the one who was baptized in 29 CE in the 15th year of the reign of Tiberius Caesar. Saul knew about Daniel's prophecy about the Seventy weeks. He knew about the prophecy that "the scepter would not turn away from Judah, nor the commander's staff, until Shiloh comes." He knew the prophecy at Hosea 11:1, which said *"Out of Egypt I called my son."*

Saul knew all the prophecies concerning the Coming Mashiach. He no doubt heard the reports about the miracles Hamashiach was performing, and how he was executed on Nisan 14, Passover night. No doubt he heard the report that at the festival of Pentecost, *about 3,000 persons were baptized that very day* – Hebrew Jews and proselytes – when Peter stood up and explained the meaning of the events that had occurred fifty days previous. But Saul had not yet made the connection between what the scriptures said about Messiah, and what Saul was seeing and hearing. Until one day the voice of Yeshua spoke to him, and everything changed. All the knowledge of scripture that Saul had, now came to life and made complete sense of who the true Messiah was. Saul's name was changed to Paul, and he spent the rest of his earthly life tirelessly trying to help his fellow Hebrew Israelites to understand what he had discerned in the scriptures.

Notice more facts regarding the original Hebrew Jew Christians *before* the foretold Apostasy took place:

- They did not use the cross nor display it in their worship. In their original writings, the original Hebrew Christians said Yeshua died on an upright stake, not a cross. The Greek word "Stauros" denotes, primarily, an upright pale or stake. On such malefactors were nailed for execution. Both the noun and the verb *stauroo,* to fasten to a stake or pale, are originally to be distinguished from the ecclesiastical form of a two beamed cross. The shape of the latter had its origin in ancient Chaldea, and was used as the symbol of the god Tammuz (being in the shape of the mystic Tau, the initial of his name. By the middle of the 3rd century A.D. the churches had either departed from, or had travestied, certain doctrines of the Christian faith. Hence, the Tau or T was adopted to stand for the cross of Christ. *Expository Dictionary of New Testament Words.* (See Notes)

- They did not celebrate "Christmas", which is actually the Roman pagan festivals of Saturnalia, and Dies Natalis Solis Invicti, which the Romans celebrated on December 25th. Yeshua was not born in December. (See Notes)

- The Hebrews looked on the celebration of birthdays as a part of idolatrous worship. Of all the holy people in the scriptures, no one is recorded to have kept a feast or held a great banquet on his birthday. It is only the ungodly ones in scripture who made celebrations over the day on which they were born.

- The Hebrew Jews and converts who made up the original Christian congregation were not split up into a clergy class and a laity class. Yeshua said to not be called Rabbi or Pastor, "for one is your teacher, whereas all you are brothers…Neither be called 'Leaders' for your Leader is one, the Christ." (Messiah) Matthew 23:8-10.

After his baptism, Yeshua spent the rest of his life on earth searching for the lost sheep of Israel. But he also said there were other persons who will need to be found:

"And I have other sheep, which are not of this fold, those also I must bring, and they will listen to my voice, and they will become one flock, one shepherd." (John 10:16)

These other sheep would not be part of his "little flock" who would rule in heaven with him. Yeshua said these other sheep are not of that fold, but they would listen to his voice and become "One" flock in unity. Who are these other sheep? In Revelation, after Yeshua's slave John counted the number of those *who were sealed out of EVERY TRIBE of the sons of Israel*, John said this:

"***After these things** I saw, and look! **A great multitude which no man was able to number, out of all nations and tribes and peoples and tongues**, standing before the throne and before the Lamb, dressed in white robes; and there were palm branches in their hands…And in response one of the elders said*

> to me: These who are dressed in the white robes, who are they and where did they come from? So right away I said to him: "My lord, you are the one that knows." And he said to me: **"These are the ones that come out of the great tribulation, and they have washed their robes and made them white in the blood of the Lamb... They will hunger no more nor thirst anymore**, neither will the sun beat down upon them nor any scorching heat, because the Lamb, who is in the midst of the throne, will shepherd them and will guide them to fountains of waters of life. **And God will wipe out every tear from their eyes.**" (Revelation 7:9,13,14,16,17)

The "other sheep" are the *Great Multitude*, who will have the hope of living here in a paradise earth! These ones do not go up to the heavenly kingdom with Yeshua and the twelve tribes, because they are not of that fold. Rather, these "other sheep" will survive the Great Tribulation while here on earth.

True Christianity, as was taught by Yeshua, is not the enemy and never was. Our enemies are *Christendom*, who is the Man of Lawlessness, and *Babylon the Great*, the world empire of false religion, or false worship. Both enemies twisted the scriptures to try to hide the truth of the Coming Seed Yeshua, whom the Most High sent.

Christendom's historical apostate record has stumbled many away from the truth revealed by Yeshua. But as was already discussed, Christendom and all of Babylon the Great, along with the wild beast, which represent the political systems of this world, will be done away with forever. Then Yeshua's Kingdom will reign without any rivals. *Soon a paradise earth will be reality.* No more hatred. No more Racism. No more pain. No more sickness. No more war. No more greedy nations fighting over control of the natural resources of the earth, such as we see today in the Congo and other countries. No more religious wars, terrorism, and genocide, such as we see now in Palestine and with the anglo-america world power in the west, the seventh head of the wild beast. The welcoming of our dead loved ones will take place here on earth in the Resurrection. Note what the Most High will soon do:

"And he will wipe out every tear from their eyes, and death will be no more, neither will mourning nor outcry nor pain be anymore. The former things have passed away." (Revelation 21:4)

During Yeshua's Millennial reign, all mankind will return to perfection, followed by the final test when Satan, the haughty rebel serpent, will receive the fatal death stroke to the head, *and the prophecy in Eden will finally be completely fulfilled*. Then the covenant that the Most High made with Abraham will be realized, which said:

"Through your seed all the families of the earth will be blessed." (Genesis 14:5)

The Most High does not hate or block anyone who is seeking to know Him in humility and truth. The Most High Yah Yehovah welcomes everyone who wishes, to follow Him by means of the arrangement He has put in place through His son, the foretold anointed Seed. The Most High has appointed Yeshua the King, to now gather all the dispersed ones, and enter the *new arrangement* for survival. The Gentile Times have ended! The Harvest time has begun!

"And this good news of the Kingdom will be preached as a witness to all the nations, and then the end will come." (Matthew 24:14)

For more information or Biblical discussion, email the author at: shankbibletalk@yahoo.com

Please also go to jw.org

Notes/Sources

Chapter 2

1. *Dynasties of Sargon. Akkad Dynasty, Sharkalisharri.* Cunniform Digital Library Initiative. http//cdli.ucla.edu

2. *Shar-Kali-Sharri, (221-2193 BC.* Universal Biography Library

3. *Petition to Bagoas*, Elephantine Papyri. Sayce-Cowley collection.

4. *The Worship of the Dead.* Gariner, John. London. 1904. Chapter 1, pg 5

5. *Life and Work at the Great Pyramid.* Piazzi Smyth, Professor C. Edinburgh. 1867, Vol II, pg 390,391

6. *Slaves were brutally branded in ancient Egypt, research shows.* Jerusalem Post. Published Novemver 13, 2022. Updated November 14, 2022.

7. Bebiankh. Egyptian king. Wikipedia

8. Nebiryraw I. Egyptian pharaoh. Wikipedia

Chapter 3

1. Gihon river. Wikipedia

2. Pishon river. Wikipedia

3. *World's First Signature – an early Biblical Name?* By Christopher Eames. https://armstronginstitute.org

4. Cuniform tablet: administrative account with entries concerning malt and barley groats. The Metropolitan Museum of Art

5. *Genetic evidence for an origin of the Armenians from Bronze Age mixing of multiple populations.* European Journal of Human Genetics, Volume 24. Published 21 Ocober 2015

6. *When Did Africans Get To Soviet Union?* (Part – 1), by Slava Tynes, *The Afro-American*, February 3, 1973.

7. *Many Africans Came To The Soviet Union During Turkish Rule* (Part – 2), by Slava Tynes, *The Afro-American*, February 10, 1973.

8. The Land of Cush. *Insight On The Scriptures*, Vol. 1, Pg 559. Watchtower Bible and Tract Society of New York, Inc. (1988)

9. Ibid, Pg 1106. Hiddekel and Euphrates Rivers

10. *The Destruction of Black Civilization*. Williams, Chancellor. Chicago. Pg 42

Chapter 4

1. Bulletin de la Societe Languedocienne de Geographie. Montpellier, 1890. Vol. 13, pg 272

2. *The Earth And Its Inhabitants*. Reclus, Elisee. Princeton, 1888. Pg 267

3. *An Account of Timbuctoo And Housa*. El Hage Abd Salam Shabeeny, collected and formatted by James Gray Jackson. 1820 Pg 187

4. *Atlas Geographus, or, A Complete System of Geography, Ancient and Modern: for Africa*. Bleau, Varenius, Cellarius. 1714. Pg 39

5. *Mission from Cape Coast Castle to Ashantee*. Bowdich, Thomas Edward. London, 1819

6. *Journal of a Residence in Ashantee*. Dupuis, Joseph. London, 1824. Pg 224

7. *Hebrewisms of West Africa*. Williams, Joseph J. Baltimore, 1931

8. *History of the Jews*. Graetz, Professor H. Philadelphia, 1894. Vol III, Chapter II

9. *Nature Knows No Color-Line*. Rogers, J.A. 1952. Pg 123

10. *The Caedmon Poems*. Kennedy, Charles W. London, 1916. Pg 101

11. *The Geography*. Strabo. Book XVI, Chapter 2, paragraph 34

12. *The Histories*. Tacitus. Book V

13. *Buffon's Natural History, Containing a Theory of the Earth, a General History of Man*. De Buffon, Georges Louis Leclerc. London, 1792. Pg 262

14. *Natural History of Man*. Prichard, James Cowles. London, 1845. Pg 145

15. Samuel Stanhope Smith, in *Freud, Race, and Gender*. Gilman, Sander L. Princeton, 1993. Pg 375

16. *Description of Guinea*. Barbot, Jean. 1746

17. *The Lost Tribes A Myth*. Godbey, Allen H. Durham, NC, 1930. Chapter 10, Pg 246

18. *Calvin's Commentary on the Bible*, Calvin, John. Comment on Deuteronomy 28:68

19. Shanakdakhete, Amanishakheto, Amanitore, Amanirenas, and Nahirqo, queens of Kush. Wikipedia

20. *The History of African Gene Flow into Southern Europeans, Levantines, and Jews*. PLOS, Genetics, April 2011

21. *North African Jews originated in biblical-era Israel, DNA analysis shows*. Reuters, August 13, 2012

22. Sulayman al-Tajir and Abu Zayd Hasan ibn Yazid Sirafi. *Ancient Accounts of India and China, By Two Mohammedan Travellers, Who went to these Parts in the 9th Century; Translated from the Arabic, By the late Learned Eusebius Renaudot*. London, 1733. Pgs 195,196. "We are assured by all Authors, both Christians and Mohammedan; and by all Travellers, both ancient and modern, that the Jews have been found in Persia…as well as Africa, not to speak of Egypt, where they have been always very numerous."

23. Eliezer Ben Hurcanus. Wikipedia

24. Pirkei DeRabbi Eliezer, Chapter 24. https://www.sefaria.org

25. *Exhaustive Concordance Of The Bible*. Strong, James. Madison, NJ, 1890

Chapter 5

1. The Merneptah Stele. Egyptian Museum, Cairo

2. Elephantine papyri and ostraca. *Textbook of Aramaic Documents from Ancient Egypt*. Egyptian Museum, Cairo

3. Family tree depicting the ancestry of the Abbasid dynasty. Wikipedia

4. From Babylon To Timbuktu. Windsor, Rudolph R. Atlanta, 2003. Pgs 88-90.

5. *Travels in North Africa*. Slouschz, Nahum. Philadelphia, 1927. Pgs 104, 344

Chapter 6

1. *Travels in North Africa*. Slouschz, Nahum. Philadelphia, 1927. Pgs 104, 228, 344

2. *History of Phoenicia*. Rawlinson, George. 1889. Book II, Chapter IX

3. The Carthaginians. *Histories*. Herodotus. Book IV. English translation by A.D. Godley, Cambridge, 1920

4. *Pseudo-Skylax's Periplus*. Translation by Brady Kiesling, from the 1878 Greek edition of B. Fabricius.

5. *Tarshish*, by Isidore Singer, M. Seligsohn. Jewish Encyclopedia.

6. *As-Sultan*. https://Temehu.com

7. *May 37 Syrtica*. Compiled by D.J. Mattingly. 1996

8. Oldest Jewish synagogue dated 10th century BCE. History of the Jews in Libya, Wikipedia

9. *Periplus of Hanno*. Codex Palatines Graecus 398. University of Heidelberg library. World Encyclopedia.

10. The Periplus of Hanno/Chapter 2. *THE GEOGRAPHY OF THE VOYAGE OF HANNO*. Wikisource.org

11. Necho II. Circumnavigation around Africa. *Histories*. Herodotus. Book IV. Translated by George Rawlinson

12. King Necho II. World Encyclopedia.

13. *Wangara, Akan, and Portuguese in the Fifteenth and Sixteenth Centuries*. Wilks, Ivor. Bakewell, Peter, editor. *Mines of Silver and Gold in the Americas*. New York, 1997

14. *The Fortunes of Africa*. Meredith, Martin. New York, 2014

15. Quote by Ibn el Faqih in 10th Century, *Mining, Metallurgy And Minting In The Middle Ages*. Blanchard, Ian, 2005. Vol 3, Pg 1127

16. Comment by Al Bakri in 11th Century. Kingdom of Ghana, Primary Source Documents, *Writings of Al Bakri (1057)*. Pardee School of Global Studies.

17. *India's Relations With East Africa: A Historical Study.* Karmwar, Dr. Manish, Department of African Studies, University of Delhi, July 2010.

Chapter 7

1. *The Two Babylons.* Hislop, Alexander. England, 1916. Pg 25

2. *Exhaustive Concordance Of The Bible.* Strong, James. Madison, NJ, 1890

3. Sulayman al-Tajir and Abu Zayd Hasan ibn Yazid Sirafi. *Ancient Accounts of India and China, By Two Mohammedan Travellers, Who went to these Parts in the 9th Century; Translated from the Arabic, By the late Learned Eusebius Renaudot.* London, 1733. Pgs 41,42,183,184

4. *Chinese Jews.* Shanghai, 1926. Pg 20

5. *The Nomenclature of Jews in China.* Loewenthal 1944. Pgs 97-101

6. *Chinese Jews, A Lecture. Delivered by Marcus N. Adler, M.A. at The Jews College Literary Society, Queen Square House, London, on June 17, 1900.* Pg 3

7. *The Survival of the Chinese Jews: The Jewish Community of Kaifeng.* Leslie, Donald. 1972. Pgs 3,4

8. Kaifeng Jews. Wikipedia

9. Jewish Entrance. Chinese Jewish Institute. https://www.chinesejews.com

10. *Records of the Grand Historian.* Qian, Sima. China, circa 91 BCE. Scroll 123. Source of the Yellow River is Kunlun Mountain

11. *Annals of the Yin, Records of the Grand Historican.* Emperor Ku's wife swallowed an egg dropped by Xuan Niao (a Black bird)

12. *Shi Jing*, (Book of Songs). The Confucian Classics. Xie, the founder of the Shang lineage, is called Xuan Wang (Black King)

13. Shang dynasty. Wikipedia

14. The Biographical Records of the Royal Mu Family. 4 Corners Of The World International Collections. Library of Congress

15. Sex and Race. Rogers, J.A. 1940. Volume One. The Nakhi tribe

16. *Says Nakhis Now Have Culture 2,000 Years Old.* New York Times, November 26, 1933, pg E8

17. *The Great Civilization Of The Kushans*, by Bobojan Gafurov. UNESCO Digital Library

18. *The Manners and Customs of the Ancient Egyptians.* Wilkinson, John Gardner. Vol.1 Pg 2. "The name of Ham is, in fact, the same as that of Egypt, Khem, or Cham"

19. *The Importation Of Negro Slaves To China Under The Tang Dynasty* (A.D. 618-901), by Professor Chang Hsing-lang, Catholic University of Peking, Bulletin No. 7, December 1930, Pgs 37-59

20. *The Magical Kunlun and "Devil Slaves": Chinese Perceptions of Dark-skinned People and Africa before 1500,* by Julie Wilensky, Sino-Platonic Papers, Number 122, July 2002; Department of East Asian Languages and Civilizations, University of Pennsylvania

21. *The Ho-ling Kuo Tiao*, Book 22, in *Hsin Tang Shu* (New History of Tang), edited by Ouyang Xiu and Song Qi (1060 CE),

22. *The Lin-yi Kuo Chuan*, Book 197, in *Chiu Tang Shu* (Old History of Tang), 10th Century CE

23. *Chen-la Kuo*, Book 10, and Book 222, Part II, in *Hsin Tang Shu* (New History of Tang)

24. *Wang Wu Tien Chu Kuo Chuan*, by Hui Ch'ao (8th Century CE)

25. *Chu Fan Chih*, by Chau Ju-K'uo (13th Century CE)

26. *Book of Jin*, edited by Fang Xuanling (648 CE)

27. *Beijing Apes Are Not Chinese Ancestors*, China News Net, January 14, 2005

Chapter 8

1. Mandate for Palestine. Wikipedia

2. United Nations Special Committee on Palestine, Wikipedia

3. Palestine: Report and General Abstracts of the Census of 1922. Government of Palestine. J.b. Barron, ed. (1923). Link (https://archive.org/details/PalestineCensus1922)

4. 1931 census of Palestine. Wikipedia

5. Village Statistics, 1945. Government Office of Statistics and the Department of Lands of the British Mandate Government. Total population of Palestine

Chapter 9

1. *Discoveries Among The Ruins Of Nineveh And Babylon: With Travels In Armenia, Kurdistan, And The Desert: Bring The Result Of A Second Expedition Undertaken For The Trustees Of The British Museum.* Layard, Austen H. New York, 1853. Pg 129

2. *The History Of Assyria, As Collected From The Inscriptions Discovered By Austin Henry Layard, ESQ, In The Ruins Of Nineveh.* Rawlinson, Henry C. London, 1852. Pgs 23,24

3. Taylor Prism. British Museum, London

4. Relief of Lachish. British Museum, London

5. *Assyrian And Babylonian Inscriptions*, by Edward H. Plumptre, contained in *The Expositer*, Series 2, Vol. II, 1881. Pg 448

6. Tel Lachish. Wikipedia

7. *The Histories*. Herodotus. Vol. 2, Chapter 36. Egyptians are shaven

8. Beard and shaving. https://www.jewishvirtuallibrary.org/beard-and-shaving

Chapter 10

1. *Annals*. Tacitus. Book 1

2. Augustus. Wikipedia

3. The *Lives of the Caesars*. Suetonius

4. *Fasti Antiates Ministrorum Domas Augustae* (Ancient Roman Calendar of Officially Commemorated Events). Appendix II. Pg 141 (Pg 146 digital version). "Augustus 17th September Deification" (AD 14)

5. *Ezra and Nehemiah: Their Lives and Times*. Rawlinson, George. London, 1890. Pgs 21,22

Chapter 11

1. *Antiquities of the Jews*. Josephus. Book 20, Chapter 9

2. *Annals*. Tacitus. Book 15, Paragraph 44

3. Gemara, Sanhedrin 43a. *Babylonian Talmud, Munich Codex* (Hebrew Manuscript 95) "Yeshu *the Nazarean* was hanged on the eve of *Passover*." (In other editions, Rabbi Dr. H. Freedman makes a footnote "Nazarean" from Munich Codex)

4. *Dialogue with Trypho*. Justin Martyr. Chapter 108, #235. Apparently on the third day the body was not found in the tomb.

5. Quotes from *The Acts of Pontius Pilate* contained in *First Apology of Justin Martyr*. Chapters 35 and 48

Chapter 12

1. *The Lost Tribes A Myth*. Godbey. Pg 218. The Expulsion of 612 CE

2. *Spain, Visigoths And The Jews*. The Incredible Story Of The Jewish People. JewishWikipedia.Info

3. *The Jews in Spain Under the Visigoths*, by Dr. Julian Furst. The Occident And American Jewish Advocate. Vol. VII, No. 8. Marcheshvan 5610, November 1849

4. *Life of Constantine*. Eusebius. Vol. III, Chapter XVIII

5. *Ecclesiastical History*. Theodoret. Book 1, Chapter 9

6. The Cross a Pagan Symbol. *The Two Babylons*. Hislop. Pg 201.

7. The Jews In Europe. *History Of The Jews*. Graetz. Chapter II

8. Senegal River (mistaken by the Portuguese for the Nile) *History of India*. Jackson, A.V. Williams. London, 1906. Pg 59

Chapter 13

1. *Christopher Columbus: His Life, His Work, His Remains, As Revealed By Original Printed And Manuscript Records, Together With An Essay On Peter Martyr of Anghera and Bartolome' de las Casas, the first historians of America*. Thatcher, John Boyd. New York, 1903. Volume II. Pgs 379, 392, 393

2. *Narrative of the Third Voyage of Columbus as Contained in Las Casas's History*. Document No. AJ-066. American Journeys Collection. Wisconsin Historical Society Digital Library And Archives. Pgs 325,326

3. *Africa and the Discovery of America*. Weiner, Leo. Philadelphia, 1920. Volume 2

4. *The Darien Indians*, by Dr. Cullen. Transactions of the Ethnological Society of London. Vol 4 (1866). Pgs 264-267. Published by the Royal Anthropological Institute of Great Britain and Ireland

Chapter 14

1. 'Unable to distinguish between a Jew from a Mohammedan.' *The Lost Tribes A Myth*. Godbey. Pg 219

2. Ibid, Pg 267 (digital page). The Fulani's belief they are descendants of Ham's son Put, or Phut.

3. Ibid, Pg 246. "Judaized Negroes were among the slaves brought to America."

4. *America, Being The Latest And Most Accurate Description of the New World*. By Arnoldus Montanus; John Ogilby. 1671. Pg 574. Jews sold as slaves to Sao Tome.

5. Two thousand children taken to "San Thome" in 1492. *The Lost Tribes A Myth*. Godbey. Pg 249

6. Ibid, Pgs 253, 255. Bishop Matthews stated his grandfather was one of the Black Jews of Nigeria.

7. *The Interesting Narrative of the Life of Olaudah Equiano, Or, Gustavus Vassa*, The African. Equiano, Olaudah. London. 1789

8. *Autobiography of Omar Ibn Said, Slave in North Carolina, 1831*. The American Historical Review, 30, No. 4 (July 1925), Pgs 787-795, John Franklin Jameson, ed.

9. *Enslaved And Freed African Muslims*. Muslim Slaves in America. Lowcountry Digital History Initiative. Ldhi.library.cofc.edu

10. Billy Simmons. Wikipedia

11. *The Gospels Written in the Negro Patois of English, with Arabic Characters, By a Mandingo Slave,* by William B. Hodgson

12. *Affairs of West Africa.* Morel. Chapter XVI, "The Fulani in West African History." Pgs 130-150.

13. *Servants of Allah.* Diouf, Sylviane. New York, 1998. Pg 280. Related account of a member of the black Hebrew community in New York who recalled certain customs as a child. (It is very possible her ancestors may have been Jews).

14. *Sweetgrass Baskets And The Gullah Tradition.* Coakley, Joyce V. Charleston, 2005

15. Judeo-Arabic dialects. Wikipedia

16. Ibid, Judaeo-Spanish

17. Ibid, Andalusi Arabic/Andalusi Romance

18. Ibid, Daggatun. This nomad Jewish tribe eventually became Muslim

19. *A Description of Timbuktu.* Africanus, Leo. 1526

20. *Half-Truths And History: The Debate Over Jews And Slavery,* by David Mills. The Washington Post. October 17, 1993

21. *Memento Mori and the Dutch and Jewish Involvement in Transatlantic Slavery.* The Jewish Museum London. https://jewishmuseum.org.uk

22. *1619 – Twenty Africans.* Hanks, Stephen. 2019. Pg 94, Map of the Congo

Chapter 15

1. *Nigeria's Igbo Jews: Lost tribe of Israel?* CNN Report, by Chika Oduah. February 4, 2013

2. *Deep in African Bush, Senegalese Tribe Claims Jewish Heritage*, by JTA. Forward News. May 26, 2013. https://forward.com/news

3. Jews in Africa. Wikipedia

4. Jews in Benin. *The Lost Tribes A Myth*. Godbey. Pg 244

5. Ibid, Pg 245. Yoruba Jews

6. Ibid, Pg 252. Jews in Jamaica and Suriname.

7. *North African Jewish and non-Jewish populations form distinctive, orthogonal clusters.* Published in the Proceedings of the National Academy of Sciences, August 6, 2012. DNA analysis shows North African Jews originated in biblical-era Israel.

8. *The History of African Gene Flow into Southern Europeans, Levantines, and Jews.* PLOS, Genetics, April 2011

9. Book of Ezra. *Encyclopedia Americana*. 1953. Vol 10 Pg 689. The Jews returned to Jerusalem in 537 BCE

10. "COMING" *Parousia. An Expository Dictionary of New Testament Words*. Vine, W.E. London, 1940. Pg 208, 209

11. John Wycliff. Wikipedia

12. Ibid, William Tyndale

13. Ibid, Michael Servetus

14. *Those About To Die*. Mannix, David. New York, 1958. Pg 135, 137. The Original Christians

15. *The New World's Foundation in the Old*. Ruth West and Willis Mason West. Boston, 1929. Pg 131

16. Early Christians in Roman Empire. H. Ingli James, quoted in *Treasury of the Christian World*. Gordon Nasby, ed. New York, 1953. Pg 369

17. Watch Tower Bible & Tract Society of New York. International Bible Students Association. *Thy Kingdom Come.* 1891. Pg 305

18. Ibid, *The Time is at Hand.* 1889. Pg 170

19. Ibid, *Jehovah's Witnesses, Proclaimers of God's Kingdom.* 1993. Pg 134, 135

20. *A Visit to the Jewish Community of Sefwi Wiawso, Ghana*, by Michael V Gershowitz. https://www.kulanu.org

Chapter 16

1. *An Expository Dictionary of New Testament Words.* Vine, W.E. London, 1940. "DOG" *Kunarion* Pg 332

2. Ibid, "PLACE" *Topos* Vol III, Pg 185

3. "CROSS" *Stauros. An Expository Dictionary of New Testament Words.* Vine, W.E. London, 1940. Vol. 1, Pg 256

4. "Christmas" The Catholic Encyclopedia, 1908, Vol. III, Pg 724

5. Dies Natalis Solis Invicti (Roman festival on December 25)

6. Date of Birth of Jesus. Wikipedia

7. The World Book Encyclopedia, 196, Vol. 3, Pg 416

8. Encyclopedia of Religion and Ethics, by James Hastings, Vol III, Pg 608,609

9. "Birthdays" The Catholic Encyclopedia, New York, 1911. Vol. X, Pg 709

10. The Imperial Bible-Dictionary, Patrick Fairbairn, ed. London, 1874. Vol I, Pg 225

The Bible Canon. The Bible is a catalog made up of 66 books, written by faithful men of God and inspired by holy spirit. The first part of the Bible, the Hebrew Scriptures, are made up of 24 books in the traditional Hebrew canon, and 39 books in today's Bible, yet they are the same exact books, due to several of the books in the Hebrew canon being placed together on the same scroll. Some editions have 22 books, because Ruth is placed with Judges and Lamentations with Jeremiah. The Greek Scriptures are made up of 27 books.

What determines canonicity? Each book must:

1. Have deep respect for the Most High's name, his purpose and his works, turning people to worship him.

2. The book must show evidence of inspiration from the Most High.

3. The book must not appeal to superstition, idol worship, or promote spiritism.

4. Each book must not conflict with the internal harmony of each other, but must be in unity with each other.

5. Each book must show accuracy, even to the smallest detail.

All 39 books of the Hebrew Scriptures (or Old Testament) were accepted and recognized for hundreds of years before the 1st Century CE. The 27 books of the Greek Scriptures (or New Testament) were established and recognized by the early Hebrew and Greek Christians in the 1st Century CE. Early manuscripts of the Greek Scriptures have been found in the 2nd Century CE proving this, such as the Muratorian Fragment dating to 170; the manuscript of Irenaeus dating to 180; the manuscript of Clement of Alexandria in 190. A few years later were found the manuscript of Tertulian in North Africa in 207; and the copy of Origen in Alexandria in 230.

An attempt was made by the Papacy of the Roman Catholic Church, at the Council of Carthage in 397 CE, to add Apocryphal books and additions, writings that were rejected for not showing evidence of inspiration or internal harmony, to the sacred Hebrew Scriptures. At the Council of Trent in 1546, the Roman Catholic Church prevailed in adding these Apocryphal writings to the Bible canon. However, those added books have been rejected by many because of the many errors, contradictions, and superstitions found therein. The one exception being the historical account of the Book of Maccabees, which is useful for historical context.

Requested Photo Credits

Adam and Eve. Mahmous Said, 1937

Map of Mesopotamia Goran Tek-en. Wikipedia

Boat of Amanitore. Sven-Steffen Arndt. Egyptian Museum Berlin. Wikipedia

Map of SE Asia. U.S. Government

The Docks at Elmina Castle. Erik B. Anderson. Wikipedia

Central America and Caribbean. Library of Congress

www.ingramcontent.com/pod-product-compliance
Lightning Source LLC
Chambersburg PA
CBHW042114100526
44587CB00025B/4047